*"The bracelet has many meanings,
you will understand more as time passes..."*

LOVE BEYOND DEATH

Barbro Curman

www.lightspira.com

Original Title: *Kärlek bortom döden*
Published by LightSpira, Sweden, 2018
www.lightspira.com

ISBN: 978-91-86613-35-8

Author: Barbro Curman
Editing & Translation to English: Jo Holmberg-Hansson

Cover Design: Ulla Lindgren & Marie Örnesved
Cover Photo Original: Nataly Tverdovskaya
Illustrations: Niklas Curman
Book Design: Marie Örnesved

Contents

— This book will be written from within. There is no other way. Therefore, you need to connect with me, as you are doing now, and exchange energies as a first stage in your writing. It will probably be so on each occasion. When you impose more traditional ambitions the flow will be broken.

Mikael's words to me describe exactly how it is. One part of me knows this, another part is stuck in old habits of doing and managing. When this happens, I start planning and controlling how the whole book will be. This immediately stops the flow, and I wonder how I will get this done.

The writing is meant to be a pleasure, I hear Mikael continue. I can't help but smile to myself. I recognise this kind of comment from our three decades together here on Earth. If there is anything I have learnt from that man, it is to pause and enjoy. That's exactly what I needed when I carried far too much responsibility inside me. Back then these comments often led me to happiness and pleasure, but also from time to time to arguments that we worked through. Uncut diamonds are there to be cut, while we are on Earth together.

Thank you, all of my guides of many kinds here on Earth and beyond, who have taught me to enjoy the great gift of pleasure! It is first now in the autumn of my life and with Heaven as my perspective for our life here on Earth, that I have understood the whole meaning of this gift. When we allow ourselves to receive unconditional love into all of our cells, we become an open vessel through which life flows. In this vessel life is manifested in earthly form through love and light. We should not interfere, just keep ourselves open. It is quite enough that we live here on Earth and wish for the highest, without having to understand.

Introduction

This book is about the fellowship of souls. Those who don't perceive that we have a soul may find reading this book a bit strange, but if you nevertheless would like to take part of my experiences and thoughts, I invite you to do so. If you would prefer, you are of course welcome to view these thoughts as only my experiences. I have no intentions of changing your beliefs. But if you are curious and longing to learn more, I hope this book will serve as a comfort and an inspiration to you.

My viewpoints have of course been impacted by my own experiences and events. Throughout these events, I have come to view life as much more and greater than merely an earthly life from birth to death. Rather that we are souls that come to Earth in order to gain earthly experiences and in that way, allow our souls to grow. I also believe that we have come here many times and we arrive in groups of "soul families". And in these constellations, we are able to support each other's development. Sometimes this is recognised as an obvious support, other times as resistance, which in turn, promotes development.

Some souls have lived many lives together and have undertaken certain common missions. They feel at home when they meet and continue developing together in different ways. An obvious relationship like that is the one I have with "my soul brother" L. We were just that, brother and sister in soul and our relationship was never a man-woman one. Our mission on Earth and also after he left his earthly life in 2003, was to build movements from a value system that we both believed in, and which was firmly grounded in society. We were inspired by the will to build a more humane world. After his death, he tapped on my shoulder from the Other Side and did not give up until I dared to listen.

14

With his help, I was taken to an inner spiritual school with one of the Ascended Masters. This experience revolutionised my life completely. I am eternally grateful for his patience when I struggled with believing in what was happening, but also with allowing the consequences of those new learnings into my life. I have written more in-depth about this journey, in my book *Head in Heaven* (2011).

During that whole period, my husband Mikael and I lived side by side at home. He was diagnosed with cancer just a few months after I had an inner meeting with a light-being who touched my forehead and hands. Simultaneously, we received our individual challenges. Our love relationship entered a new phase, as we were both on our individual spiritual journeys. We talked about this and came to call it "being each other's garden". Love is to allow the other to develop and to the best of your ability, support and contribute to your partner's development.

My Other Half

The above is an old expression or idiom that has survived many centuries and reflects experience and wisdom. What do we mean by it? Everyone has their own interpretation, of course. To me, this expression is about the union of souls, and in this way I sense Mikael as my "other half". What I mean by this will be made clear by this book. Before, when we were both alive and living together, I had some inklings about the vastness of our souls. All that I have experienced after Mikael's passing has made me feel peaceful, safe and securely connected in spirit, to Mikael in his new place, and also to all that exist in higher frequencies.

Along the way I have sought confirmation for my experiences as they have felt too big and important to deal with on my own. Now, I feel I rest safely in his soul's arms, while simultaneously living my life here on Earth.

Mikael and I met during the summer of 1981, and immediately at our first meeting, I was taken aback and very surprised by my own reactions to him. I heard how I silently said to myself: "I cannot pass by this man! Even though I don't know what kind of relationship we will have, it is clear he will always be an important part of my life." We each had a marriage behind us and were both wary about believing in love and our abilities to create a long-standing relationship between ourselves and our respective children. Already then, in the middle of our strong passion, there was a deeper part of him that was the deciding factor for me, and to him, that feeling was mutual.

So, we had thirty-one years together, during which we became a family together with our children from both our previous marriages and our common son. The family now consists of six children, eight grandchildren and four great-grandchildren. It is such a great joy to grow together, enjoy each other's company and all other aspects of family life. The entire clan was there in the intensive care unit on the day that Mikael said farewell to his big family. Grief and sorrow but also warmth and humour existed side by side on that unforgettable day.

Mikael and I were colleagues and worked as Gestalt Therapists, with individuals, groups, and couples. Above all, we examined the man-woman relationship in great depth, by working together as a therapist couple, with couples in need of help. You can hardly imagine a more effective way of 'cutting our diamonds'. When working with couples as we did, authentically with ourselves as instruments, it was impossible not to, simultaneously having to deal with what those processes surfaced in Mikael's and my relationship. Throughout our years together we continuously worked on and evolved our relationship, but did so "in private quarters". I realise now, that all this has been an important preparation for the gift we now have received. The gift of experiencing unconditional love across dimensions.

Amongst the most difficult things to cope with, when Mikael could no longer share my life here on Earth, was being without all our wonderful conversations. We used to sit in the living room on opposite couches talking, many times for hours. We could always talk about absolutely everything and did so too. My, sometimes slightly wild, life that entailed starting a new business every tenth year or so, was made possible through Mikael's and my common ground and understanding, in which I could rest in between my endeavours. Mikael was the philosopher who liked to be at home in peace, reading and writing. While I, as the leader, took care of busy and sometimes also messy situations. Together we became a whole in this, as neither of us wanted the other's role. My desire to build up new things and be in the centre disappeared with Mikael, when he died. His decisive role became clear. And I went into stillness, continuing working, but in a completely new way.

Mikael died in March 2012 after having lived more than seven years since receiving his lung cancer diagnosis. The unity of souls that I have felt since his death, is beyond my comprehension. I understand now that my book *Head in Heaven* was a preparation for that which I have now experienced. I perceive that time, as if I was on a spiritual boot camp, and a very concrete one too. Without those experiences, I would not have been able to welcome Mikael in the way I now can.

Energy and Frequency

Throughout this book you, the reader, will learn how it can be to meet another person's soul while you, yourself are still here on Earth. Quite often expressions such as energy and different frequencies will be used. It's not as mystical as it may sound. It was through my inner school described in *Head in Heaven* that I came in touch with these types of experiences and received help in stabilising and strengthening them. It is similarly whatever you choose to practice, like meditation, music, reading or anything else. What you focus on and put energy into, soon become a natural part of your life. It has been like this for me with this sort of energy, as well as for many others that walk similar paths.

If you want to delve more deeply into this aspect of yourself, there are several possibilities. For example, Reiki, Kundalini yoga, Chakra meditation and so on. I have not done any of this myself, but would have chosen to do so if I had known what it would have given me. On the other hand, as a Gestalt Therapist, I have been trained for decades in bodily awareness, training of the senses and mindfulness. "Eternity is in the now", it is said and I agree. I am very grateful for all I have learnt through this training. It has been crucial for the gift that I have now been able to experience.

The energy I speak of in this book is a kind of electromagnetic energy that surrounds and fills everything. Today there are photographs of auras. Our subtle senses register this energy. Some people can see this energy, some hear it and others can feel it as sensations in their bodies. Some can also detect it with their thoughts – suddenly they just know. The most well-known way is to see auras. I can't do that at all, rather I sense a presence or hear beyond my physical ear. I can get inner images and dreams, but I do not see auras or other phenomena in physical space.

The so-called Kundalini power, the current of life, which is available to all and that is best developed under supervision, came spontaneously to me about twelve years ago. I got help to stabilise and live with it. By this inner work I developed the so-called "light body[1]" which in its turn is in contact with other energy bodies. It was through these practices that I literally experienced that the physical body we wander around in here on Earth functions as a sort of "cape" while we are living here. It is returned to the Earth while our energy bodies live on in timeless dimensions. It was a great gift to have this experience behind me, when I followed Mikael through his death.

If we assume the thought that we are souls who are here on Earth for earthly experiences, then it is not so strange that we consist of different frequencies of energy, where physical frequency is the slowest and the densest one. Even the physical frequency consists of energy. We are not as dense as we imagine ourselves to be. Both the micro and macro cosmos reveal this. Frequencies of energy are all about numbers of vibrations somewhat like octaves on a piano. While we live in the third dimension of time and space, we observe certain patterns of frequency/vibration. These can be expressed as light or sound, or perceived as impressions.

---

1) The" light body" is a concept in many spiritual paths. Some call it the "etheric body". Amongst the Egyptian mystery schools, the light body is named as "Mer-Ka-Ba". It involves developing a flow of energy and light that weave together the physical body and dimension with other dimensions. This is achieved by meditation linked with the Kundalini force and the different chakras that are within our human bodies as a potential. In Egyptian mythology Ka is the energy body closest to the physical body and is also linked to Ba, the soul, which is in turn connected to several higher energy bodies. See: Padma Aon Prakasha: *The Nine Eyes of Light* and Drunvalo Melchizedek: *The Ancient Secret of the Flower of Life*, volume 2.

Some people are born with a special sensitivity and can perceive frequencies beyond the earthly dimension. This gift can have its upsides and downsides. Children with this gift, often believe that everybody can see and perceive in this way. The rest of us that do not have an obvious gift can still train our intuition if we wish to. It is often a life crisis that opens us up to the idea that life is something more than the reality that exists here on Earth. It may be the death of a relative, a disease or some other extremely challenging situations.

Many more than we think have this kind of sensitivity, but repress it. During all my years as a therapist I have met many in my consultation room that have experiences of their loved ones from the Other Side. They have even described experiencing light phenomena, light beings or angels. Unfortunately, most of them have felt it necessary to keep quiet about this experience which has been one of the most significant part of their lives. They have been afraid to be ridiculed or to be patted on the head as if they had only created these experiences in their imagination, for comfort during grief or to escape from a horrendous situation.

Traditional science considers that the brain creates these inner images and experiences. Newer alternative and high-quality research goes against this tradition. The brain is seen as a receiver of information rather than something that creates it. It picks up stuff from "the cloud" as they say in IT. This comparison is quite good. A few researchers in this area speak of "The Zero Point Field", that is to say a field of potentials that we connect with by resonance.

My bewildering inner experiences have led me to try understanding what happens in my inner self. My intellect sought confirmation, understanding and people who had experienced something similar. I have always avoided anything that resembles a sect or cult, nor have

I felt a need for my experiences to be analysed or understood through any religious affiliations. When you keep an open mind, wisdom comes in just the right amount for us to assimilate.

Throughout the years I have consciously sought advice regarding the same questions from several spiritual guides. Independently, they have seen that which I have felt and heard. Tangible things like books falling from their shelves just at the right time to further my learning and so on. Today I do not need these confirmations but they have been crucial along the way.

The current spiritual life that has become mine, is about meeting soulmates in friendship. We can exchange experience, support one another and feel the power in a small or larger group. I do not prefer so many fixed groups. Every meeting provides inspiration to each of us and this pattern repeat for many in our society. This force does not generally show in public, but many well known people in society take part beneath the surface. The time is coming soon when experiences such as those I describe in this book, will be completely natural.

There is a tale, a story of a man who came to an island where everybody had lost their physical vision. He had his intact. When he came to the island he described what he saw. The people became very angry with him. They thought he was lying and making it all up. He was completely alone in his perception. Nobody believed him. In today's secularised society many people react similarly to experiences beyond the physical reality.

Why this book?

Just as when I was about to start writing my previous book *Head in Heaven*, I have felt anguish about starting to write. Now I am ready, but there has been both fear and longing along the way. Some of you may think, why not just let everything be my own experience and leave it at that?

When I wrote *Head in Heaven* I did it for two reasons. I had discovered what I had longed for all my life, but I was nonetheless afraid to be open about it. Therefore, it was necessary to go against my own fear. It would have been impossible and deceitful not to stand up for everything I had discovered. My other reason was that it could give something to others who, like me, had suppressed this gift. The world really needs unconditional love, such as I had the joy of experiencing. That love is out there, waiting for everyone. It should not be hidden away.

I hope that *Love Beyond Death* will be an inspiration and comfort to you and to those who have lost their loved ones. All the signs that people in the midst of grief are especially open to, are important to take seriously. Love is what connects the worlds. It is not about trying to keep our loved ones here on Earth, nor about avoiding getting on with our own lives. On the contrary, it becomes possible to have a breakthrough by gaining access to more dimensions than this one we currently live in.

This time my reticence has mostly been due to the fact that I am writing about more than just myself. Mikael is my husband, but he is also a much-loved father/stepfather, grandfather, brother, uncle and friend. Everyone has their own relationship and story with him. So, I asked and was answered. As our youngest son so aptly put it. "You are writing about your *own* experience mum! It's quite okay."

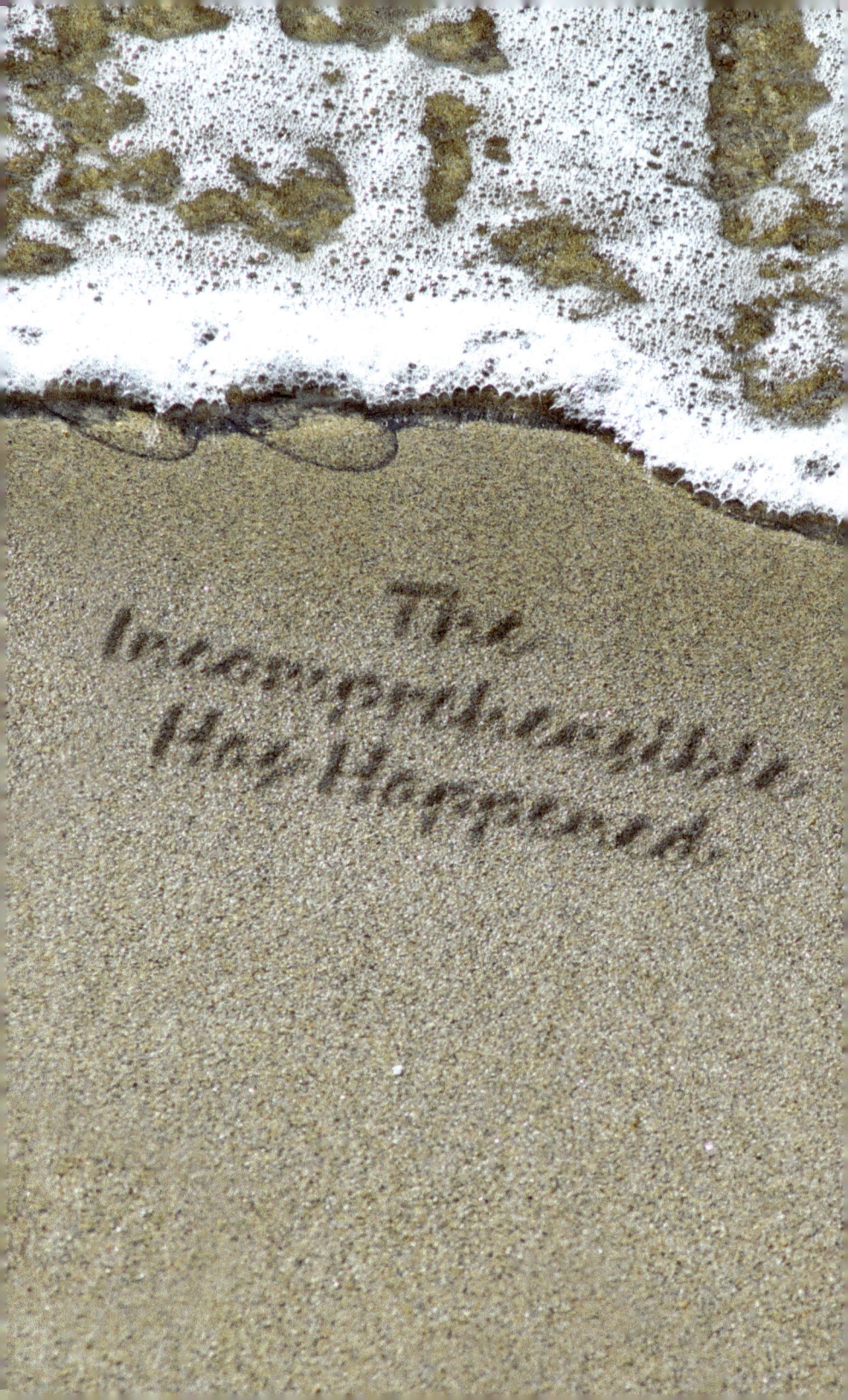

Today is Easter Monday and I am sitting here at home on the sofa. In front of me is the large photo of Mikael and me standing happily together in the water by our summer house. We are both smiling. A candle is lit in front of the picture and the room is filled with beautiful flowers. I have never ever received as many flowers as today, when the man in my life has left this worldly existence.

Outside the birds are singing, spring is in the air. A while ago a large red bird came into the house. I opened all the doors and windows to let it out, but it stayed inside the kitchen. I've never seen a bird of this kind before and absolutely not in the house. To me, the presence of the bird felt like a greeting and it was important, I felt, that the bird should have its freedom. When it couldn't find its own way out, I chose to pick it up carefully in my hands, to let it out. Strangely enough, it seemed quite calm there in my hands and made no resistance. To me, it was like speaking to Mikael, he, the most freedom-loving man of all men. "Fly and be free", I said to the bird and helped it through the kitchen door.

At some point, I had said the same to Mikael, in one of our many silent conversations: "I feel your presence and your energy, but I absolutely don't want my grief to pull you down energetically, preventing you from being wherever you are". As quick as lightning and in a wave of energy, some words appeared *You cannot!*

This is a special Easter Holiday as it is a little more than two weeks since our whole family said our last farewells to Mikael. We were about twenty people in the intensive care ward, both young and old, and all close family. Mikael made sure to speak personally to each and every one of us. We were there together for several hours. Sadness and tears were mixed with laughter. Mikael's humour was constantly present, even in these moments of farewell.

That same morning, we had found out that there was nothing left that could be done for him. When I met him in the morning, he knew and was prepared. The night had been demanding for him, but in the morning he had had some intense experiences, which in some way had shown him the path ahead. We were both amazed that we could share that precious moment.

To me, it was difficult to admit that this powerful man soon would die, even though he had to use an oxygen mask to assist his breathing. While we all sat around his bed, he suddenly sat himself up and made a speech, coming from deep within his heart, addressing his love for life and life itself.

— Go out and live your lives and do not allow yourselves to be limited!

To us all, but especially to the young ones present, he shared his love of life right there in his moment of death. He told us that he was grateful and happy for his life, that his body was worn out and that he was prepared to die. It was obvious that he wasn't scared.

Mikael lifted his oxygen mask up and he and I gave each other the last kiss. He thought it was worthwhile even if his lips turned blue from this short absence of oxygen. That kiss stays with me as our last kiss here on Earth. After that, he lay down and it looked like he was preparing himself to die. But it wasn't his time just yet. With his amazing humour, he said:

— Death does not come easily, I don't know how to die.

And this made us laugh, right there in the midst of all sadness. All we could say was that we don't know either.

Still, I felt this probably was a sign that he was too tired to have all of us around him, it was exhausting to him. He and I were then left alone, but it would still take an additional ten hours until it was time for his last breath. During this time, I felt prepared to forget my own grief and fly away with him. Silently I asked my inner guides to be there for him when his soul left his body, and with their help, I felt Mikael and I were on a bridging wave of energy. This process lasted into the night, and the nursing staff kindly brought me a bed so that I could be close to Mikael. It felt good to be able to lie beside him one last time and it reminded me of the thirty years that we had been sleeping side-by-side.

Towards the end, Mikael's sons came back to visit. First, the eldest came, and as a physician, he was able to help his dad when he was in pain. Later, the younger brothers arrived as well. When I think back to these last hours, they very much felt like birth in reverse. Right then it was as if Mikael was being born into another reality, while at the same time, the breathing in his physical body became more and more infrequent until it finally stopped. In many ways, a dead body is so extremely dead! How quickly it becomes an empty shell, how quickly life leaves it! It was a strange feeling to return home, to leave this body that I knew so well and to go home with only a bag of his clothes and other belongings. But with no Mikael.

That evening, Mikael's sons and I got together, and the following day all the children and I gathered in Mikael's and my home. Together we tried to make sense of what had happened. Of course, we couldn't. Rather awkwardly we made waffles and put the garden furniture out. It felt so strange to do these routine things without Mikael. Sitting in the garden, we slowly started to make initial plans for the funeral.

Now, two weeks later, I sit here in our home, trying to understand what has happened and out of habit, I take out a notebook. For at least eight years I have kept a diary to record my most inner feelings and thoughts. It has helped me and strengthened my experiences. This time there is a gap of three weeks since I last wrote. The events around me have been so turbulent that I haven't been able to write. But now it's possible again, and I'm writing about this intense, sad, but still so special, period.

My perspective has already shifted and at the soul level, I understand so much more about the purpose and meaning of Mikael's and my life together. I find myself viewing old events in a new light, and hence new patterns emerge. Today it's clear to me, that throughout all those years when I was trained to be able to absorb energies and unconditional love, Mikael was in stillness at home, keeping us both grounded. He gave me the necessary foundation and at the same time, I gained knowledge and experiences which are now of use to us both. Back then, I realised some of this but couldn't see the whole picture. Now I am seeing and understanding more and more, and slowly beginning to realise that as souls, we are on a common mission.

Last weekend memories from our first time together emerged. Memories of falling in love and experiencing Mikael's enormous unyielding power as a man. That power became totally free and open in the moment he finished his life, in love and for life. I found myself experiencing our initial feelings of falling in love, all over again. His love came to me with full force and filled my heart completely. Along with that force of love, I was at the same time overwhelmed by grief, missing and longing for his warm embrace. On the other hand, I still didn't feel alone, as I was surrounded by our souls' energies.

In the afternoon of the Good Friday, I was watching TV, when a powerful wave of energy came into my body via the upper part of my head (the crown[2]) and went straight into my heart. I was shocked, as I could feel Mikael's presence. It was a completely new form of energy than I had previously received from my inner spirit guides. Mikael came through with the same powerful masculine passion that I had experienced many times here on Earth. This passion was combined with totally free and unconditional love, such love that few are capable of while incarnated in physical bodies. That moment marked a turning point as it made me understand that Mikael and I could still meet, but now on a soul level. All this was happening at the same time as I was mourning my late husband. I learned that the closeness in souls did not reduce my grief, quite the contrary. Still, I got to feel the love relationship of our souls, which I hoped and believed would develop and deepen.

A few days before Good Friday I had heard a voice inside my head. It was one of the inner guides who had been with me for many years and through whom I have been given unconditional love. He encouraged me by saying:

— *Your old spiritual symbols for connecting are not needed any longer, instead they are now manifested within. With the help of this unconditional love, you will meet Mikael on the Other Side. It is happening through you and him at this moment.*

---

2)   The most widely known chakra system describes that we have seven or eight chakras available. This is analogous to an octave on the piano, where the first and last become the eighth. The Egyptian system has twelve to thirteen chakras where the thirteenth is the first and last tones. Drunvalo (see below) compares this with the chromatic scale, that is to say all the keys on the piano including the black ones. Personally, I recognised myself in the Egyptian system since in that two heart chakras are described, one for universal love and one for personal love. This helped me to understand what was occurring in meeting Mikael after his death. For more information, see Drunvalo Melchizedek: *The Ancient Secret of the Flower of Life*, volume 2.

Two years ago, I was told by my spirit guide, *Love with our kind of love*. And since then this unconditional love has been pouring through me. The day following this, Mikael invited me to come to him as a woman after a break of several years. How could he have known of the changes that just had happened within me? In turn, I invited him back the following day.

Apparently, these two events completed the process that able our current closeness. They were not so much about traditional sexuality, rather an exchange of energy. Now, two years later, I understand why this happened as it did. It laid the basis for the way we are able to meet now, on a soul level. This combination and integration of unconditional love and earthly love are possible only when earthly restrictions are removed. I realise now that this love-integration is the key to why we can meet across worlds.

On Easter Sunday, there was another inner meeting between Mikael and me. A voice inside me said:

— You need to raise your own energies if you are to meet Mikael now – so that you don't pull him down by your human longings to be with him.

And so, it was. I laid still and spoke to his soul. I told him I was prepared to be his vessel here on Earth and that I absolutely didn't want to pull him down. At that point, a beam of energy shot with full force into the middle of my heart and chest. It was right there in the centre. Earlier I had received energies a little to the right of my heart and in a much milder way. This time the energy continued and I was elevated into a higher energetic frequency. It was a solemn meeting as man and woman in this new energy. We were united in spirit. The fact that we had lived together on Earth for such a long time as husband and wife, made this experience all the stronger.

When this joint energy-bubble started fading, I realised that several hours had passed. Peace and calmness followed. I was laying on the couch, surrounded by all the flowers from the funeral, trying to make sense of it all. How was it possible to feel so happy and satisfied during these inner soul-meetings, while at the same time feeling such deep pain because the man in my life was no longer physically by my side?

How would I cope moving between these two completely different states? Slowly I felt my perspectives becoming so much clearer. I understood that this was merely the beginning of a path that had been prepared for a long time. When looking back, I realise these preparations had been particularly obvious during the last seven to eight years of Mikael's and my life together. Yet still, in an infinitely bigger picture, these preparations may have been going on for many lifetimes. Whatever time would mean at the soul level...

Later during Easter Sunday, a close friend came to visit. She is one of those friends that had helped me so wholeheartedly with the practicalities of planning Mikael's funeral. We made a beautiful brochure with the words that Mikael had written by hand during his final days in hospital. He had new insights about life then, due to the limitations he was placed under, being completely dependent upon his oxygen mask and fighting to reverse pneumonia in his one remaining lung. It was urgent for him to spread this material. Therefore, it was important that this brochure was made available to all attending his funeral.

Easter Holiday is almost over and tomorrow I will venture out into the world again. I have decided to continue working, which will be possible by the caring support of my closest colleagues. It's almost a paradox, but working and being with colleagues will provide a kind of emotional sanctuary in which I will be able to function, at least a little bit. It will help me in some way to continue my daily life, feeling almost as if all is still well and Mikael is just at home waiting for me. I found this to be my way of coping with the grief, dealing with it in steps, with breaks in between.

Two weeks passed since the very special Easter Holiday and it is four days until Mikael's funeral when family and close friends will be able to say our last goodbyes. These past two weeks have been filled with intensity and it has felt to me as if I'm living two completely different, parallel lives. One life has been about concrete and practical preparations for the funeral and the other life has been about a deepening of the inner soul-meetings with Mikael, in which a new kind of love-relationship has begun to emerge. I am amazed and grateful this is at all possible. I wouldn't ever have imagined anything like this, not even in my wildest imagination. Inside of me, I silently thank my spirit guides who have prepared the ground, helping my energies to elevate to necessary levels for Mikael and me to meet in spirit.

In the early morning after the Easter weekend, I had partaken in a third spiritual connection with Mikael. It was the first morning I felt completely calm inside since his death. I was taken aback by how unyieldingly strong and full of love he was in spirit. The recurrence of these meetings gave me a sense of security.

It was as though we had learned to connect to each other's energies in an obvious and natural way. It was also clear to me now, that there was no risk of me energetically "pulling him down" out of my longing for him. The many years of spiritual training I had received, seemed to make sure this didn't happen. My sexuality had been transformed to intensive love energy that Mikael and I could share at the soul level.

At one point, I asked Mikael if it would be a hinder to our spiritual connection, if I viewed him as the man who had once been my lover. *Dress me in whatever image you like!*, I heard. In that moment, I did not need to, just enjoyed feeling his amazingly strong and loving energy just as it was. *The mountains are coming together!* I heard myself say. These words came from the depths of my soul. And I knew that they were about our common mission here on Earth. To me, it was as if an inner pattern had become clear or apparent to me, concerning my journeys to Tibet, the Andes and later to Egypt.

During my earlier spiritual training, the so-called Ka or Light Body was created within me. What now has happened during my soul-meetings with Mikael, is that it has been possible for us to meet in our light bodies, meetings that have been deep and passionate. It felt as our light bodies became more entwined with each soul-meeting, and that this closeness in soul was united with our long life together as man and wife. A new kind of love-relationship was emerging and deepening.

During our soul-meetings the Kundalini force was fully flowing within me from a wide-open crown chakra and third eye and all the way down to the root chakra. The energy was flowing both ways and my skin became extremely sensitive. The energies were high and tingling and I felt like an electric organism. These energy flows lasted a vast part of the night. I found them to be very vitalising and that they help me cope with the other part of my life, with my grief, and the loss of my "physical husband". At the same time as I was wide open and very close to Mikael in spirit, the pain of not being able to be in his arms, became even greater.

One night before Mikael's funeral, we had a new inner soul-meeting. It was characterised by extreme intensity, heat, and stillness in each second and it happened with a power more intense than I ever could have imagined to be possible. It was as if I was flushed by these energies, along my entire spine and throughout my body. My feeling at that moment was that our energies became completely united.

Now we are married in spirit, I heard in my head. And so it was. In that moment, I understood more deeply why I wanted the symbols of Mikael's and my flower wreaths at the funeral: They were similar to what we both wore on our jackets when we were married many years ago.

The day of the funeral arrived, and I found myself at church. All our family and so many of our friends are there to say our final goodbyes to Mikael and his life on Earth. Outside, spring has arrived. The coffin, which is at the end of the aisle by the altar, is covered in beautiful flowers. The church too is overflowing by flowers, wreaths, family and friends, it is very beautiful.

We have chosen to place the coffin in the aisle so that it can be right beside us. I am sitting to the right of the coffin, with our youngest son on the other side of me. At this moment Mikael's presence is so strong that it feels like he is on my left. Consciously I know that his dead body is lying there in the coffin, still I feel his presence so very strongly.

Thirty years ago, Mikael and I were married at our home. Instead of a bridal bouquet, we both wore identical buttonhole-flowers shaped as wreaths, made of pink rosebuds. Today I have a similar one pinned to my black suit jacket. A similar wreath of pink rosebuds is placed at the front of the coffin. When the funeral is over I will bring it home so the two wreaths will be united again.

Details like this are so important to me right now. They are like an invisible conversation between Mikael and me. I also communicate by the way I dress. I have a black knee-length skirt and black dress jacket to mark my grief. Under the jacket, I am visibly wearing a raspberry-red blouse to symbolise that love is eternal and that it lives on inside of me. I know that Mikael can read and understand my messages and agrees.

As I sit there in the middle of Mikael's funeral I feel the energy boiling in my heart. He is here in soul and spirit while his body has become an empty shell, lying in the coffin by my side. Although feeling his soul's presence, it feels very important to say farewell to the physical man I was married to for so many years, and all who are here have the same wish of saying their heartfelt goodbyes. While all this is taking place I also know that Mikael is present at another level.

The music helps us say our goodbyes, it has been carefully chosen by us. Family members and friends are also contributing and performing in different ways throughout the funeral. I am happy that Mikael's soul can listen to the music as it always has been important to him. Especially during later years, he and I united around Leonard Cohen's song Anthem. A male choir consisting of family friends performs it now, in a fashion that is close to Mikael's taste. He enjoyed singing and did so using his powerful and beautiful voice. To remind me of Mikael's voice during the first days after his death, I filled the house with Pavarotti singing. It was a way for me to cope. Pavarotti's masculine voice filled my heart and made me feel Mikael's presence.

I am overwhelmed and grateful to see all these people walking up to the coffin to pay their last respects and how they all, on their way back, give me a hug. To me, it feels as if they all first greet Mikael and then me, it seems natural and the right thing to do. Still I feel Mikael's presence so strongly that it is almost tangible. How can we be here together, when I know that his dead body is lying in the coffin? Nonetheless, all of us who hug are also crying. All those people are like an invisible embrace that helps me and the family during this transition.

After the funeral, we all move to the Parish House and a shared memorial. There is food, mingling, more singing, and there is a table with Mikael's books and publications.

A slideshow covering his life is also running through-out. I got help printing Mikael's last thoughts from the hospital bed, and they are now available in the form of a booklet, for our friends and family who are present. While the slideshow tells about Mikael's life, a few of us say a few words from our hearts. It is a bright memorial. This is so, because it is held for a man who was prepared to die and who was grateful for the life he had had and lived. Now it's up to us who are left behind, to live our lives in the same ways.

Food and drink were always important to Mikael and we say our farewells in the same spirit as he would have liked. After the memorial, some family members and relatives end the day together with a spring buffet at our house, exactly what Mikael would have wanted us to do. A close friend of mine has come to stay and sleeps in Mikael's bedroom. This all helps me with the transition. A few of us eat breakfast together the day after the intensive day of the funeral. I am so grateful for that, as this is the time when the loneliness starts creeping in...

When everybody has left my home, I walk alone among the abundance of wreaths and flowers taking pictures with my mobile to preserve the memories. The house feels very empty and I am not feeling any spiritual connection. Mikael's and my inner soul-meetings do not take away my sadness, but they do give meaning to my existence. I feel lost during these days after the funeral and I am wondering whether the experiences I have had of inner contact now has ceased? I place a beautiful silk scarf with butterflies over our large dining-room table. It helps me to accept how things are. On the piano, a row of photos is placed, photos of happy times and wonder-ful togetherness as a couple and family. On the table, I have placed the large photo of when we are standing in the water outside our beloved summer house. This is my favourite photo of us. How will I ever be able to say "I" and not "we"?

A few days later I am in the garden, resting in a sun chair, enjoying the first warm spring day. I need many hours of stillness each day, for everything to sink in. I feel an enormous gratitude to all my friends who have been there for my family and me in so many ways. They have provided a warm and safe shoulder to cry on and helped us keep going. While I have been laying there in the sun, I have allowed myself to be carried off to another realm, and Mikael and I have connected once again. I love feeling reconnected to our souls' foundation, which from now on will be growing stronger and stronger. Having this strong connection established, was also making me feel safe. Our wreaths or rings of roses in front of the photograph serves as a symbol of this soul connection and this confirmation makes me feel happy and safe again. I reflect how strange it is being tossed between strong feelings of longing and grief and strong feelings of connection, closeness, and love.

The emotional roller coaster became increasingly more intense during the months following Mikael's death. I found myself being thrown between states of soulful joy and amazement and states of deepest despair. Now, two months after Mikael's departure and one month after the funeral, I'm starting to realise that the only thing life is about, is dealing with various states of consciousness. I'm so grateful for my long spiritual and psychological training, which have taught me to observe myself in various now-moments. My theoretical and philosophical training, including all my years of applying this in my work as a psychologist, have taught me that we are not our feelings, not our bodies, nor our thoughts. Still, what I'm now experiencing in a turbulent real-life way, shakes the very foundations of my life and is sometimes overwhelming to take in or deal with, despite my years of training and preparation. This new learning concerns the very basis of life, it's about the tangible existence of the soul and about being able to perceive other dimensions and worlds. Dimensions, that to me are as real as our earthly reality. In this new learning, everything becomes clear, concrete and necessary for me to relate to.

During this period, I am sensitive to how people around me view life and death. I find myself living more and more by myself and in my inner world. To me, it feels as if my inner world makes up the major part of my life, still I feel unable to speak to others about it. When people ask me how I'm doing, I find myself giving a watered-down summary of what is going on. I express my grief and I also add that I can feel Mikael's presence, which seems hard for many to relate to, and they often say something like: "It must be a comfort to you". They mean well, but it hurts anyhow. How can I possibly explain that due to Mikael's and my soul-meetings and closeness, the pain of not having him physically near me, is even greater? Still, it is true that his presence gives me great happiness! This is one aspect of what I call The Paradox of Life.

To millions of people on our planet, the fact that we have a soul is a given. Many also know that we all are souls who are here to gain worldly experience and that it is possible to communicate between worlds and dimensions. To me during this vulnerable time, it is a great relief to meet people who also find this completely natural. In such company, I'm able to relax and to be comfortable sharing my entire life, without having to censor my words and hide what happens in my soul-meetings with Mikael. This softens the sharp differences of my life's two dimensions.

Some of my clairvoyant friends were not present at Mikael's funeral. Instead, they took time wherever they were and connected clairvoyantly to the event. After-wards, they shared their experiences with me. Their perspectives stretch common perceptions of what is possible and what is not. To me, it was a great gift which helped me integrate the different worlds within me.

Some of what they said then, I still keep in my heart. Several of my clairvoyant friends had, completely inde-pendently, seen Mikael as a Tibetan monk in one of his previous lives. To me, this felt very special, as I once had a similar experience of Mikael when he was alive. This happened many years ago when Mikael and I were meditating together. In my mind's eye, I saw Mikael as a Tibetan monk, with bright humorous eyes.

The vision of Mikael as a Tibetan monk was confirmed a month before his death, by another clairvoyant friend of mine. She described seeing Tibetan monks in orange robes, wandering about in our garden. At that time, I didn't connect to the orange colour nor did I understand the meaning of what my friend was seeing. But now, after Mikael's death, it makes sense. It became clear that the monks, Mikael's brothers, were showing themselves as a sign that it soon would be time for them to accom-pany him to the Other Side.

Another clairvoyant friend, who was following Mikael's funeral from her home, said afterwards:

— He told me that he had had many lives, both as a leader, preacher, and monk etc. Through you, he has learned what love is. So, he went straight up to the Light, floating on a beam of light. Even though he wanted to meet his brothers, he went straight up.

Now, I understand what my friend meant. The love Mikael has received through me is the overflow from the love I have received from my inner guide, Master Kuthumi. All this occurred during the last few years of his life when Mikael and I were on our independent inner journeys. I realise now, that it's as we are being able to combine our different spiritual traditions, which have had different impacts on us and which has been made possible through our inner soul-meetings. What a gift this is!

The Buddhist/Tibetan tradition has purified *wisdom* in its teaching. That was so apparently Mikael's path. Even as an adolescent he was called "the philosopher" by his friends. He loved to sit for hours looking out over the sea, twirling his hair. Stillness, silence, and timelessness were inspirations for him. Despite all this, he was a person who liked good food, parties, and long conversations about life. He could be quite unruly and rebellious in his desire to be free.

While we lived together, our inner soul experiences were slightly different. Mikael drew his inspiration in stillness, nature, and in certain kinds of music. On my part, the experiences came through my body as hearing and images. "Do you have to be so concrete," he said to me many times, although he was always very accepting.

The Christ tradition stresses love to all creation. The first time I experienced this was as a four-year-old when I heard a voice, but no words, and felt the presence of Jesus Christ. I did not mention this to anyone until I was thirty years old and had met the person I call my soul brother, L. It was he who, after his death, came "knocking on me" and brought me to Master Kuthumi's etheric retreat. For five years, I was awoken early every morning and was allowed to, as an inner journey, take part in the Master's teaching, wisdom, and love. Almost every night I absorbed the energies that came to me, wrote, slept a short while, and then went to work[3].

This knowledge has made me understand why I've always have had such strong impulses to travel to Tibet, Peru/Bolivia and Egypt. Many years ago, in my inner listening, I had heard: *The mountains are coming together!* I understand that this concerned many levels and dimensions. The mountains are the Himalayas and the Andes, which represent different spiritual traditions, and Egypt is like the heart and the synthesis between these two mountains. These three spiritual traditions are about purifying wisdom and love respectively, and through this synthesis, they are now able to come together[4]. To me, this is the parallel for how Mikael and I are united in spirit.

The great paradox, after Mikael's death, is that the intense and unconditional love that we now can share, wouldn't have been possible if we were both in earthly bodies. While alive, we humans live mostly in the world of dualism and linear time. We struggle with fears that obstruct our abilities to both give and receive unconditional love. I believe the meaning for us humans to even

---

3) If you would like to read more about this, please refer to my book *Head in Heaven* (2011)

4) Please refer to Drunvalo Melchizedek (2007), *Serpent of Light*

be on Earth, is to make it possible for the soul to experience these extremes, and hence have the opportunity to develop.

Through my inner schooling with Master Kuthumi, I learned to be able to receive unconditional love and to develop the so-called light body. There is nothing so provoking as this kind of love that exists beyond the personality. It melts down our defences. Now it is Mikael who is the light-being and who gives me this kind of love and I am able to receive it thanks to the training I had from Master Kuthumi.

To experience such soul-meetings with my beloved husband is mind-boggling. At the same time, it awakens a huge desire to be able to experience this love physically between us, to feel his skin and find me in his arms. The soul-meetings fills me with love and happiness, but after a while, the emptiness and pain of him not being here takes over. The paradox expresses itself!

At some point between Mikael's death and his funeral, I woke up in the middle of a wonderful energy transfer. I recognised the kind of energy, which I call the Holy Spirit and have felt before. Through this energy my body opened up from the heart to the throat. The heart expanded as well. Then I saw a flash from the past dissolve in love and I heard Mikael speak to me.

– *Now I'm able to give you all my unconditional love. It has been there all along, but my earthly blockages prevented me from giving it to you when we lived together.*

I received this beautiful love into all my cells and became soft and warm. I answered him, that during the past years I also had learned how to receive this kind of love. Both of us have now learned this. I then felt how the energies became even higher. A deep cough that I had struggled with, was softened up and dissolved. Filled to the brim, I heard Mikael again:

— *To think that we can meet like this – me up here and you on Earth. I understand that you needed to go away and be by yourself when you learned this. It is a gift to us both!*

I felt happy, warm and light, and a feeling of harmony ran right through me.

Another time I found myself in a completely different state. Even though it still felt empty, I was now able to enjoy the spring and even to relax a little. At that time, I was longing to feel Mikael's and my souls' closeness once again, but knew that this couldn't be forced, it would happen when it happened. The cough in my upper chest and throat had returned and it awoke memories from a Past Life. I perceived the cough as a sign that intense love energies were at work, melting away old blockages in the body. The release of these old patterns came later, in the form of nausea. Old rage was passing through my body and made me shiver. I could feel this intensely in my solar plexus area.

The Past Life that was emerging was about abandonment and betrayal in love. My feelings were that Mikael and I were a couple in that life as well, but at that time I made myself into a victim, giving up on life. As a consequence of this, I have found it difficult to deal with people who play the victim role, and have instead taken on the role of the one to blame, even though this seldom was true. Understanding the dynamics of this past life, gave me great insights into my current life. In the same way, this is how we humans often balance different polarities and learn through the experiences of many lifetimes. When I have got these insights and understood them through body and soul, the blockages were released.

My mental state shifts like this from day to day in the roller coaster of life. One evening I was sitting, watching a mediocre television show. Suddenly, a powerful beam of energy came in straight through my head and went further down through my spine downwards and upwards at the same time. I was taken aback as it made me shiver, and released old sadness and tears that had become stuck inside. I felt it was Mikael coming and giving me the power to be able to be in the middle of my grief and at the same time receive these high love energies. I sat there for a long time, shivering with sadness and receiving love simultaneously. It was a rather strange combination of contradictory emotions but it allowed frozen parts of me to "defrost". Afterwards, it was time to wrap myself up like a cocoon in bed and make sure I kept really warm.

Another night I received a loving message from Mikael, through a special dream. In this dream he came flying horizontally into the room, landed in front of me and kissed me passionately in front of other people. There was a special quality about this dream as well as about another one that came soon afterwards. They were nothing like ordinary dreams, but felt like a message from him. Mikael was showing himself in his most vital age and in both of those dreams he was flying.

In this way life went on, blissful heights and painful lows. Now, when one month had passed since Mikael's death, I can see that I have been living in our house trying to understand what has happened. I've spent many hours of grief, experiencing our home echoing with emptiness. Why isn't he there in his usual place, on the couch opposite mine? Why don't I hear his cheerful voice when I'm back home from work? Why aren't his arms around my shoulders, something I loved since the day we met and why am I not in his warm embrace? It is so difficult to realise that he is not with me in physical form any longer. Still in the midst of missing him so deeply, the grief is replaced by those wonderful soul-meetings, which are so utterly tangible and real.

After a completely wonderful session with one of my clairvoyant friends, I am sitting in the garden allowing all those new insights and feelings to sink in. I had asked my friend to guide me and give me her impressions regarding Mikael and me. She and I haven't met for several months as she couldn't attend Mikael's funeral in person. It is a relief to be seen and understood through my friend's clairvoyant views. As soon as we met, Mikael "took over the stage" completely. My clairvoyant friend described him as an unusually powerful and clear soul.

— *I'm fine here, but it's still a bit unfamiliar,* was the first he said to her.

He expressed how happy he was, that I had been able to accompany him in spirit, when he crossed over to the Other Side. He then continued:

— *Good that she (Barbro) was so stubborn, insisting that there are other worlds – and now I am here! We have never been closer to each other than now!*

My clairvoyant friend saw the funeral before her inner sight. She described in detail how the church looked, and she even saw Mikael's soul attend his own funeral, taking part in everything. That coincides with my impressions from the church, but I never "saw him", I only felt his energy.

And the music…. it built bridges between the worlds … my friend said, referring to the powerful music being played at the funeral. "Exactly – Pavarotti," I thought to myself then…

At home, there in the sunny garden, I think about the fact that there are only a few people who can see and understand clearly how it is to live with this great life-paradox. When I met my clairvoyant friend earlier today, I was so grateful and appreciative of her understanding of the delicate balance that characterise my life at the moment. On the one hand, she understood how I'm experiencing being cut in half, since Mikael isn't here with me any more. On the other hand, she was also, in a quite natural way, able to confirm the new soul-level love relationship between Mikael and me. Living with these polarities is extremely demanding, but it also gives me a great sense of purpose for my life. I understand that my life is about co-creating and thereby contributing to a more humane world. I sense that this is just the beginning of a long inner journey, which is about creating a completely new life together with Mikael, with him on the Other Side while I remain here on Earth.

My task is to be available and open to all that might happen, and to stay open, even if I am not able to understand intellectually what happens each moment. I sense that at this special time on Earth, there are more couples who cooperate between the dimensions, for the common good on Earth.

Spring continues as if nothing has happened. That's how life is for me, as I live in a kind of a bubble. Almost three months after Mikael's death, I have started to approach the outside world in more ways than just going to work and meeting my family, both situations that have helped me cope with my grief. Still, the last weeks have been demanding for me. I have learned to keep my inner energy-pillar stable, living from that energy in the midst of my grief, being careful not to lose myself in grief nor deny it. Also, there has been no way for me to escape to Mikael's and my soul–meetings. If I try to initiate them myself they won't emerge, as these soul-meetings are completely beyond my control. The only way for me to cope and keep from being overwhelmed is making sure I live my life precisely in the present.

During the last week, I have participated in a conference where I also facilitated one of the seminaries. This seminar had been planned a long time with Mikael and me as lecturers. A close friend, who knew Mikael well, was there with me instead. I could have cancelled, but it felt important to live through the situation, and with this support it went well. However, when it was time for the third and final day of the conference, I was overwhelmed, feeling I could no longer cope interacting with that many people. Instead, I decided to stay home, and I spent the whole day outside in my garden. Even though the conference was very inspiring and worthwhile; solitude was necessary and I realised how fragile I still was.

Earlier in the week of the conference, I had attended a family funeral, as one of Mikael's uncles, after a long illness, had died just a couple of weeks after Mikael. I wanted to attend the funeral but it was painful to be there with the whole family present and without Mikael by my side. Despite being surrounded by love and support, I felt like just half a person, and that my life rested on rocky grounds.

Maybe this in all was too much for my system and I got unbalanced, or maybe I had to meet my inner shadows. It was like I needed to encounter all the nooks and crannies from all of Mikael's and my years together. Looking back, I feel as if everything needed to be brought to the surface and to be reconciled in love. While all this was going on, I found myself time and time again, struggling with doubts about Mikael's and my souls' love-relationship. Despite all confirmation and assurance I had received, I kept asking myself, is he really there on the Other Side?

That same evening I felt out of balance and strange things started happening to Mikael's computer, which was in his study switched on, but with the screen saver running. The computer started acting in ways I had never experienced before, flipping between ordinary screensaver-pictures and new patterns and pictures I had never seen before and which felt like messages. Earlier during the evening when I had been so very tired and sad I had pushed away what was happening on the screen. It was like I couldn't cope taking in anything additionally. I felt nauseous, angry, and sad, lost in self-pity, I cried and cried…

After a while, I pulled myself together, asked for inner guidance and I received help. Later when I walked past the computer, I saw new pictures. There were very strong images about our planet and what is happening to it. First, I saw a completely dead planet, which to me was a sign that I was supposed to use my power and contribute, followed by powerful symbolical images that were full of life. Towards the end, in the middle of the night, special words were shown on the screen. They were in Latin so I looked them up in a dictionary. They meant: "Making or requiring Atonement." In my current state-of-mind, I was doing just that, reconciling. I realised the messages were about Mikael's and my life together on Earth. About healing hurtful things, we both occasionally had done to each other, but also about Past Lives that all of a sudden began to emerge.

And then: *You are with us, even though your body is on Earth.* These words came several times, and so it is. My mission is to keep this bridge open, a completely bare bridge[5] where I stand in the middle all by myself. "My Swedish name means bare bridge", I said to some English-speaking colleagues at the conference. At that moment I finally understood the meaning of my name and what my life purpose is.

"I'm gathering everything horizontally and everything vertically to a single shivering NOW." This is how I described what I am going through to a close friend. The horizontal is Mikael's and my years together as a physical couple and the vertical is our new loving relationship between dimensions. Everything is surfacing to be reconciled through unconditional love. It is a powerful and breath-taking transformation in all dimensions, necessary for the mission we have taken on. This transformation also includes Past Lives that come up to be healed through love.

While I process and heal, my energies are being raised so that I can enjoy new loving soul-meetings with Mikael. I'm gaining wisdom about how this is happening, and I can see patterns emerging. I realise that I need to release my feelings in order to be healed. I also understand how necessary and important it is to pray for help. It is as though the link between the dimensions is becoming stronger through the trials I have faced. At last, I understand that Mikael and others on the Other Side are there the whole time and that I am the one who breaks the contact when, like this time, I get lost in self-pity. Sadness

---

5) The author's name, Barbro (a Swedish form of the English name Barbara), can be split into the two Swedish words bar + bro which in turn translates into "bare bridge".

is one thing, self-pity another! The risk of breaking the contact is also greater when I am too tired and don't' listen inwardly, or when I allow negative thoughts, either internal or external thoughts, to take over.

Now I am at home, we are at home! My soul's bridge to the spiritual world has become so wonderfully strong and compassionate. I can fully trust it. Being in this state of mind requires raising to higher frequencies. There is nothing new in that, it's just a strong reminder. After that moment, I spontaneously looked into Mikael's wardrobes. For the first time, and with this feeling inside of me, I was able to touch his clothes without being overwhelmed with grief.

The same evening, I sat down and enjoyed a good movie, *Among Us*, a Swedish film from 2010. At the end of the film, "the angel" walks around and addresses "you" and tells "you" that the first rays of the sun are "you", that all of life's beauty is "you". When I looked up, the moon was shining outside as if greeting me. It was the first quarter of the new moon.

The first summer after Mikael's death I spent by the sea, in our summer cottage on the Swedish west coast. This place has been Mikael's corner of the Earth, ever since he was a child and it has become mine and ours together. It is a very powerful place, situated on the beach with the sea right outside every window, bringing in all kinds of weather to our doorstep. Behind the house is a very tall cliff formed and shaped by stones and gravel from the Ice Age. Every moment here is like living on the border between the Earth and the Universe.

This summer, the personal and the heavenly heart within me, merged very tangibly through my soul-meetings with Mikael. What happened was strengthened when I, in my mind's eye, saw him everywhere in and around our summer cottage. The place where we had spent so many summers together, but this time he was here in spirit instead of in his physical body. Moments of missing the physical closeness were healed by the knowledge that his physical body would not have been able to be here this summer. Something that would have been a painful loss to him. Now he was here in soul. Our children and grandchildren, who joined me at different times throughout the summer, seemed to have the same feeling. He was alive and present to them too. Time and space didn't exist. All was one in love.

A few weeks before I travelled to the summer cottage, I visited one of my clairvoyant friends. During the session she offered me, she relayed Mikael's words very concretely: *Our hearts are now alchemically united as if carved in gold.* While I was listening to her reading, I did not understand the entire depth and meaning of the words Mikael was sending me. Later, in the light of what had happened during this special summer, including all the soul-meetings with him, the picture became clearer and I felt as if Heaven and Earth were merging within me. In that light, what had begun in the months after Mikael's death, when I was being torn in a storm between the pain of grief on the one hand and the joy of our soul-meetings on the other, now gradually melted together into one heart. A heart that was "we" and which, at a soul level, was holding the two of us.

The merging of our two hearts happened in waves. Just like one morning, when I was alone in the house and still in bed. I was enjoying the feeling of freedom and never-ending time, when suddenly I heard knockings from the next room. Repeated knockings that were quite clear and loud. At the same time, I felt how a gentle and power-ful beam of energy entered the crown of my head, like a clear visitation. The knocking sounds were loud and my impulse was to get up and check who was out there. A voice inside me calmed me down and I stayed where I was, surrendering and receiving a silent and lovely energy exchange between Mikael and myself, all at the soul level. *Wonderful things are short – love vanquishes death and all that happens!* These, his words, I heard within me.

Later that evening, when I was sitting on the same bench where Mikael and I so often sat together, viewing the entire sea in all directions, I heard a voice within me saying: *Fly now, little dove!* I heard these rather unusual words several times, and I was not able to tell whether the words were coming from Mikael or my inner Master Kuthumi. It wasn't the usual way Mikael would have expressed himself, when he was here physically, but so much was different now.

What I did know was that I was not yet prepared to fly. I cried and cried and realised that I, for the time being, was not ready to face the world alone. I sat there on the bench for a long time and after a while I was consoled by a gentle inner spiritual energy, reminding me that I was not alone after all. I felt consoled and a was relieved within. Just at that time the horizon became brighter and

I felt as if nature was mirroring my feelings which were no longer so dark. Deep inside, I knew that my life would get brighter too and that a lot was waiting for me in times ahead. I also knew that Mikael and I, as souls, had made this agreement a very long time ago.

The awareness of our golden heart, created out of love and living inside me, was showing me the way. After the tough moment at the bench, I went to bed and fell asleep quickly, but woke up in the early hours of the morning. Inner pictures of myself in earlier relationships, before Mikael, were passing by my mind´s inner eye. At the core of these pictures were the theme of abandonment and loneliness, a theme that Mikael and I when we met, both brought with us into our relationship.

I went back to bed and made sure that I was warm and well tucked in. As soon as my head hit the pillow a warm beam came directly into my neck (my proud neck!) and in this beam, I gratefully felt Mikael's love for me. The heat from the beam was spreading to both my heart chakras. It began with the heart chakra on the right-hand side, in which I for a long time had been receiving the Universe' love through Master Kuthumi's aura, and it continued into the heart chakra in the middle of my chest – the place for receiving the personal love on Earth.

"You are reaching into my innermost corners," I said to Mikael, as I understood that I needed to receive his love into the depths of my physical body by being in precise awareness, allowing his spiritual energy to enter my body second by second. While this was happening, I could see in my mind's eye, his symbol for me, which related to the rose wreaths that I had given us at his funeral. In the process, old blockages were gently released while my "light hands" were joining both my heart chakras together millimetre by millimetre. This was a wonderful, and at the same time relaxing, experience. I enjoyed feeling how a deep energy was spreading, mostly up towards my throat but also downwards into my body. I asked all my cells to absorb this energy!

Love with our love!, I heard from Mikael. I had heard these same words two years earlier from Master Kuthumi when I had learned to receive the same kind of unconditional love as I was now receiving from Mikael. At the time two years ago, I gave the love I had received on to Mikael and we joined in it together. This time, the same kind of heavenly love was coming from Mikael and was merged with his love for me. It was created through the unification of both our heart chakras, the Universe's love and the personal love. Who would have known?

The summer continued this way, melting together sadness and longing on the physical level, with increasing love and closeness at the soul level. The web between the worlds often seemed to merge, many times by the great help of nature and the elements surrounding me. The nights were filled with these lovely energies and both my heart chakras were filled to the brim.

Early one morning I was awoken by a voice. It was Mikael who said; *My little dove!*. He would never have said this on Earth and I asked him if he was part of Kuthumi's Cosmic family as these words were closer to the way Kuthumi had been speaking to me. *Yes, just like you and L.* Mikael answered, and continued;

– *Now you carry our golden heart in your physical body, a great responsibility. You can always turn to our heart in your physical body, just place your hands there. Then you have the right focus. Understand now that this is the frequency that will be sent out into the world. Your most important mission is to hold this, our frequency. Therefore, you must not distract yourself with such that lowers the frequency. We depend upon you being in our frequency.*

Suddenly everything became so clear and simple, and at the same time so huge. My path became obvious, as I understood that my source is the whole time our golden heart. With this source of spiritual energy within me, I will be able to contribute in creating situations, networks, environments, where these frequencies can vibrate for the good of people. In the manner I was spoken to, I could recognise Kuthumi's decisiveness from all the earlier teaching I had received from him. *Do you understand now? ...*

In my physical body, the region above my chest – the thymus – had become so alive and vibrant. The golden heart had created a powerful and yet gentle and loving space there. I got to know certain points on the body that are crucial for the flow of this spiritual energy throughout the body. I decided deep inside: "I will buy a beautiful golden heart and have a ruby set in it as a link, a sign." Ruby had since many years had a symbolical meaning to me in my spiritual life.

One morning, when the summer by the sea was drawing to a close, I heard the following words:

– Now it is about merging the highest and lowest frequencies within you – merging Heaven and Earth. You are getting much more sophisticated at doing this after the long training.

The words were accompanied by a soul-meeting between Mikael and me as a way of illustrating what was happening. I was grateful to get this understanding and I got a new perspective to what one of my clairvoyant friends had told me three years earlier. "Continue to do your light work exercises!" she told me back then. At that time, I was wondering what was going on, but to her, it had been self-evident, without me even having to tell her in words.

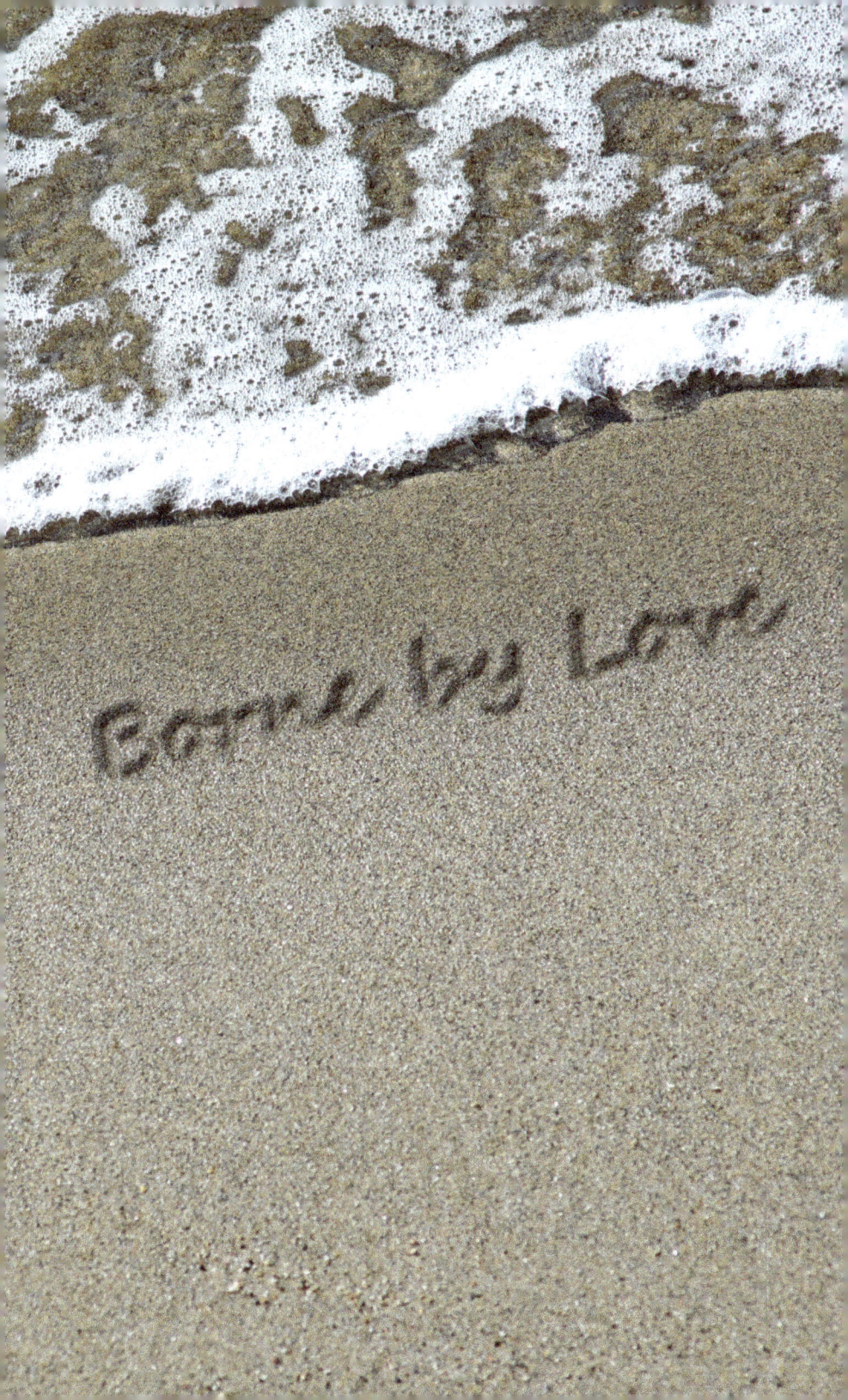

At the summer house on the beach, staying close to the sea, the earth and the sky help me to slowly begin a new kind of life after Mikael's death. The veil between the worlds disappears and the dimensions become woven together in the presence of those strong forces of nature. My inner journey continues and since arriving at the summer house I have been receiving strong guidance around what this life is about and the ultimate purpose of me remaining on Earth with Mikael on the Other Side. I'm so touched and grateful for all this loving inner guidance!

My relationship to Mikael in his new dimension has been building up strongly during the summer, making our connection at the soul level feel very powerful. Still, I am struggling with the fact that the foundation, which my physical life rests on, feels brittle without having Mikael physically by my side. On arriving back home to Stockholm at the end of the summer, I have a hard time feeling at home because of all practical things that need my attention. I find myself amidst planning inheritance, putting the house on the market and in the process of going through all that belongs to the history of our long life together, living in the house. I have decided to sell the house. I know, for several reasons, this is a necessary step for me to create a new life, nonetheless I feel lost, tired, and sad.

As I so often have experienced, I receive help from above, to carry me through the most difficult passages in my life. This help arrives and begins within my own physical body, and eventually makes me realise that help has arrived, emotionally and at the soul level. The extreme tiredness and urine infection I suffered from during the first weeks after the summer, I see as a form of cleansing. One day during this time, I fell asleep right after coming home from work and slept for almost two days! This was not a normal sleep but rather a state between sleep and meditation. When I woke up after these two days it was as if I had awoken to a new life. My strength started returning. I felt as if I, during these two days, had been carried up to Mikael's dimension. Up there, in those loving energies, I could rest and recover.

During this period, I also organised a seminar at our house together with my good friend Justo Viscarra, who is a naturalist practitioner, trained in traditional Bolivian medicine. Without any effort at all there were fifteen participants, open-minded people who easily could allow Mikael's soul to be included in the seminar. With the help of the participants and Justo, the energy of our house was transformed so that it corresponded to the new reality of Mikael not physically living there. I understood that this was made possible thanks to other dimensions being present and active in this transformation. Immediately after the seminar, the energies in the house could flow freely again, without any blockages and I could once again feel that I could breathe freely. I felt as if I had been empowered to take over the ownership of our house. By fully owning our house and caring for it, I am now able to put the house up sale and set all of us that own it free. There is much love for this house from so many, both family and friends. I need to take my time, be gentle and thank the house for all that it has given to us. And I am not alone in this. Everybody who considers our house their home, needs to take their time to say goodbye.

It is now the end of August and five months since Mikael passed away. In my world, time can be divided in "before" and "after" this crucial event. I wonder if I will ever think differently?

The very day after what I call the cleansing of our house and myself, I have one of those lovely mornings. Mikael came to me in a new way, which I understand had become possible as I had raised my energies through the cleansing process. These moments always arrive unexpectedly and beyond my control. The only thing I have found is, that if I am trying to control these lovely moments of contact, they definitely do not occur. This morning, I am relaxed and Mikael and I meet in an intense, calm love between Heaven and Earth, and it feels like bliss. My body became completely soft. The energies blended and I heard amongst other things:

– *It is this that is the purpose and our mission. It is easy for you to get in contact with me like this, and so we can meet. We carry these soul-meetings with us wherever we are. Heaven needs Earth's energy and the Earth needs Heaven's. Your body has been cleansed to make it possible. Joy and pleasure in love.*

Similar soul-meetings came a couple more times as if to confirm the connection and for me to really understand. Now, at the end of August, I can live from this inner platform that has been given to me. It helps me to cope with all the outside things that need to be taken care of. On my way home from work, one day in late August, I stopped by the goldsmith's to exchange a gold chain. Instead of my old one, I chose a twisted one in white and yellow gold. The twisted gold chain represents so well the last week's soul-meetings between Mikael and me. That, and the heart itself, are a confirmation of this new step we have taken together. To me it is also a way to communicate with Mikael, across dimensions.

I return home, and realise again how wonderful it feels to come home, and how much I enjoy sitting in the garden. When there in the garden, I become very aware of how strongly the sun shines, warming the top of my head at the same time as my lower back becomes extremely sensitive. To me it all feels like a greeting. Calmly, calmly, second by second I allowed myself to be filled with these high energies. An infinite tenderness came to me through Mikael, as if to show what love really means. I allowed myself, step by step, to receive what I experienced as a caress on my cheeks. Then, a powerful stream of words came to me:

– *Do not doubt now. These are words from your husband. Receive them! And the necklace is really from me to you. I cannot physically go into shops now. I led you there. The time was right!*

To me, this soul-meeting is so memorable and special as it also meant I learnt a lot. I am beginning to understand how various energy centres in my physical body are interconnected to my inner experiences. It is not easy to describe this to others. It feels very private. Luckily, I have discovered some books in the esoteric literature that describe what I, or we, are experiencing and this gives me a sense of perspective, increased understanding and a deeper meaning[6].

---

6) Please see Padma Aon Prakasha's modern interpretation of the ancient Egypt tradition: *The Nine Eyes of Light* (2010), *The Power of Shakti* (2009) & *Womb Wisdom* (2011)

The journey to Peru and Bolivia is drawing closer. It is part of three spiritual journeys that I three years ago decided to undertake. At the time I heard a voice tell me *the mountains are coming together,* although I did not understand the deeper meaning of those words then. I only knew it involved the Himalayas and the Andes, but no more. Since then I have been inspired both from within and through books that have "turned up" just at the right moment, but back then I had no idea what those words meant.

After arriving home from the summer house, I found ordinary life extremely demanding while living a completely wonderful life in my inner world. Keeping myself together in these circumstances requires on the one hand discipline, and on the other hand the ability to let go. It seems contradictory but the fact is that the one depends on the other. The inner training, I undertook during the years before Mikael's death has led me to be able to live in this way. Only now, the intensity of it is all the greater.

In the external world I am the leader of a small consultant company. These colleagues are so much more than an ordinary working group as our fundament comes from the heart and skills beyond traditional competence. I am proud of the work we do and I care about the group for the best of us all. However in our society, this kind of work has become increasingly tougher. There are issues to take care of before I leave. Still it is a very responsible team and I am learning to let go more and more.

In the earthly world, I also have to deal with all the details of selling Mikael's and my home. Ever since I felt empowered to take over the ownership of the house, I have organised those things that need to be done before the winter and my journey to South America. I am careful not to make any decisions at all until after the trip.

I am more and more aware that big changes are about to happen in my life and that I should be prepared for anything.

In my inner world, Mikael keeps coming to me intimately and lovingly. He arrives in a straightforward manner and with clear messages. Sometimes he is very forthright and places his words directly on my tongue, but mostly I just hear his words in my inner mind. Lately, at times, another Light Being has been accompanying Mikael on his visits. This Light Being arrives with another kind of energy, very different from what I feel from Mikael. This other energy is what I call Christ energy and is a very gentle energy that reaches into every cell with its strong love. During these times, I feel the Christ energy expresses its blessing to me and us both.

A common thread in the messages is that I need to be prepared for a completely new sort of life and that Mikael and I have a common mission, a mission we once upon a time chose together and for which we now are being prepared. Part of the preparation is our inner soul-meetings where we meet in energy and blend our light bodies. During these soul-meetings, there is no distance to speak of, all is just one in love. When I look at the pattern of our inner soul-meetings the past month, I understand why the intensity has been so great. We need to have advanced our learnings before it is time to travel to South America and most importantly, to Lake Titicaca.

About a month after I came home from the summer house I took a trip to see my sister. The night before the journey was intense. It was one of those occasions where Mikael placed words on my tongue. In the morning, I could not remember all the words, but it was about the importance of living in faith and love and thereby being able to hold the frequency so that he and I could be very close. This helps me a lot, especially when it comes to getting through the uncertain and anxious periods I am experiencing in the external world.

The close and intense soul-meeting continued after breakfast the following morning – my whole body was shaking and felt like it was dissolving. I did not feel solid and it was as though my cells were floating around in a sea of gentle, soft and gorgeous love. A couple of hours later I had to cope with a troublesome train journey which was a really abrupt change.

During my journey, Mikael came to me in the most surprising places, on the train and right among other people. It was as if to demonstrate that the place is unimportant. Right there on a commuter train, I heard his words pour out:

– *You should now be prepared for a completely new life. Anything can happen. Our light bodies are now woven together and react together. Get ready to travel. You will understand more after the trip (to Peru/Bolivia).*

A couple of days later, on the train home, it was as if I was embedded in a bubble of energy, and in a state between meditation and sleep. The morning's inner soul-meeting was still there with me. I was starting to recognise a pattern in these soul-meetings. High energies come in through the crown chakra. These energies connect with our shared heart that now lives within me and which vibrates at the same frequency as the crown chakra's energy. The same high energy goes through the light column down my spine to the base of my back and as a woman, I am touched by a calm, intimate pulse.

During the same morning, very high, shivering energies passed through me. I felt an embracing heat that flooded every cell of my body. The soles of my feet came together and kept this flow within my body. I have never felt such a sense of security and closeness. My physical body became a vessel for our intimate union in our light bodies. Traditional lust and sexuality are no more. It has transcended into this intense light. Nonetheless, it is our underlying love and passion for each other that has made this possible.

The following days I felt such an inner peace, which made it so much easier to get on with all the practical matters that needed my attention. These inner soul-meetings have helped me stay receptive to high energies. A complete surrender in faith and love – and I was in the most loving hands. Sooo grateful and amazed! During these days, I got this message:

– *Love creates – it takes place at the molecular level in these high energies.*

Gradually I experienced more and more inner soul-meetings which all raised our energies. On one occasion, I entered another state of consciousness and experienced an ancient ceremony. The ceremony unfolded step by step, all directed from inside by Mikael. It was like melting together. I fell asleep glowing, embraced and happy. The morning after this ceremony other light beings came and gave their blessing to our union.

Certain days I could feel some hesitation about leaving the house. The contrast between the earthly things we humans must deal with on a daily basis and the miracles I have had the gift to experience in my inner self, had begun to affect me. One day, when I felt like this, I allowed myself a gentle landing at work, enjoyed a nice lunch together with good friends, and made sure just to complete the most urgent tasks at my office. Still, those feelings of being torn between my inner and outer life worsened, when I later during the day went into the city. Finding enthusiasm and joy was hard. I almost didn't want to be here on Earth at all – or, I thought to myself, maybe what I need is to create a completely new kind of life!

On the way home, a gentle beam of energy went through me and warmed me up. Thank You! A voice said:

– You've just felt how most people feel with all the stress and pressure that goes on in people's lives. You have the privilege of living in these high, loving energies and have learned how to stay there. Most people do not know how to and need you to show the way. To understand the difference and to have courage. This is the purpose of your work, and it's not about traditional business at all.

So true! I recalled different situations and meetings when I have seen the strong longing within a person or the members of a group. And how important I've always felt it to be, to acknowledge that longing! I realised that in all of this I am privileged. That it is up to me to make sure I create a life based on what I am now. Everything else seems pointless…

The preparations for the journey to Peru/Bolivia have intensified up until now, a few days before leaving. Putting it in perspective, I understand that all these inner soul-meetings in energy have been for this purpose. The greatest challenge lies in me having to be in two worlds at the same time, having to be that "bare bridge"[7]. At the same time, I understand that this is just the point and purpose of my life. The message is clear – it is about building a completely new life. What that means I do not know. To me, my task is making myself pure and free so that this new life can be created within me, the rest is beyond my control. I surrender to the higher powers for this to happen. From within me, I am required to say yes or no to continue walking this path. Surrounded by loving energies I confirm that I am ready.

---

7) A literal translation of the author's Swedish name Barbro, into English, would be "Bare bridge".

On such an occasion Mikael suddenly entered my light column along my spine. It was joyful to meet him and to receive his powerful spirit and energy. We met and our light bodies melted into one. Just as usual Mikael's words came from my left and placed themselves on my tongue. I had asked him how he is doing and where he is:

– *All my different layers of "shell" are gone. I am free! Love is the most important thing, that we can be joined like this in love and that we can make a difference through our union. I wish to thank you for allowing and being able to maintain our union in your physical body. It is unusual, but there are many couples like this nowadays. Make sure that you don't get tied down, we need to be able to fly together. You are so careful and conscientious when finishing up and organising all the old stuff. That is good and what we need to do. When everything is done we will be even freer. You should surround yourself with people that understand us so that you feel safe in the physical world, as well as in the inner world where we have each other. Our light bodies are conjoined forever. I love you, little dove! I would never have said that on Earth, but I say it now. Enjoy your day at home. It is nice to have a couple of quiet days. We need that!*

Our wedding anniversary was drawing close. It was going to be very different from previous years. The preparation came the day before in that Mikael reached out to me very decisively, with the words:

– *Be prepared – nothing will be the same after the trip! The energy that is being created from our inner soul-meetings strengthens and builds our light bodies, which are being melted together. It is from there we can create – everything.*

He made his point clear by making my left hand grasp the right hand and holding them over my ovaries.

— *This is our focus from now on – on our union. Everything comes out of that. So, keep the focus like this with your right arm and hand, so that you don't get distracted by other activities elsewhere. You must be free now.*

The day of our anniversary arrived. I was very caught up in work that day, and my mind was absent when passing by a flower shop on my way home. A couple of cerise pink gladioli called out to me and I bought them without reflecting that it was our wedding anniversary, which only occurred to me in the car, driving home.

That evening the flowers provided a beautiful display while I was talking to Mikael by his photograph. We were also celebrating our new marriage between souls. Later that evening we held a loving ceremony between Heaven and Earth where we thanked our spiritual guardians.

The anniversary marked a turning point in my outer life. I could now more easily live from our inner life and out. I became freer about where I wanted to live in future. Most important was to be free and not tied down at any level. So much had happened within me. Mikael's words the weeks before he died came to me again and again: *I am grateful! I have had a good life.* It became clear that these words were true even for me. My whole life has been good, but particularly the time I had together with Mikael has been so, and I know that the feeling is mutual.

After our anniversary Mikael surprised me by coming to me in new ways during our inner soul-meetings. This helped me cope with everything that needed to be done by me personally, as I was still responsible for everything practical. One evening a couple of days before the trip and during our soul-meeting, a powerful energy sphere was built up. Then his voice was there, centred on an area in my throat, which was throbbing: *We are now one voice. Be prepared!*

The area around my throat chakra was connected to the other chakras with a clear pulse between them. Before everything was connected all the energy went to the area behind my navel, which is linked to the universal love (which in turn is beyond our personal love). I heard Mikael declare quite concretely:

— *What you have ahead of you is greater and more different than you can imagine. A completely different level. Finish off what you have thought about and then let go. The journey will be life-changing. Anything can happen. You do not have a normal life ahead of you. We fly together and speak with one voice.*

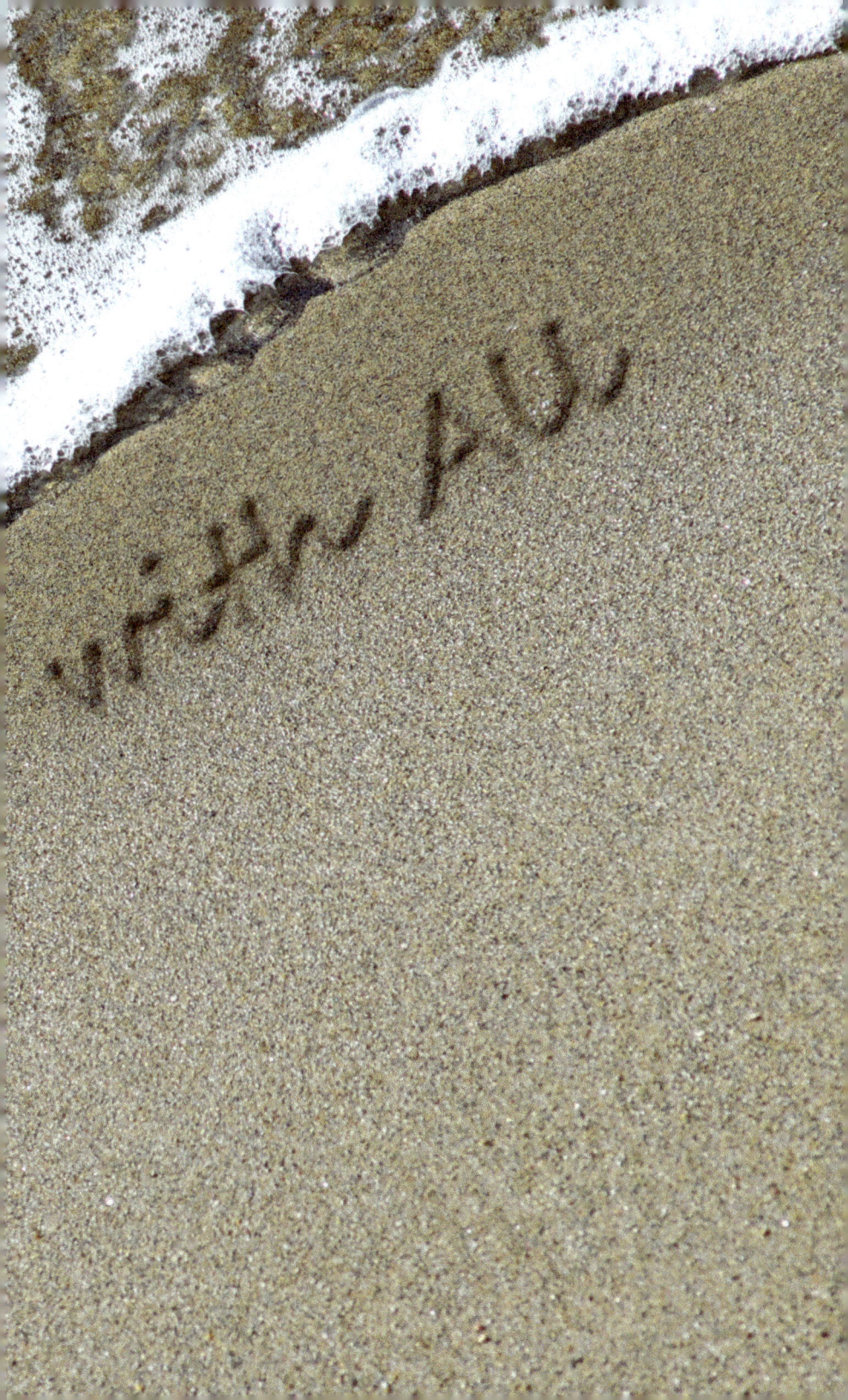

The day before I left for South America, I visited my clairvoyant friend Doris. It felt important to get a second opinion from an independent medium, after this period of intense emotions and life-altering experiences. During the session, Mikael immediately appeared, powerfully and with humour. He expressed that he was happy in our union, that he had chosen to be a part of this. He joked about how practical it was that he in spirit was coming along on this trip. He described how many hours he had sat in our house and longed for me. Now we are closer than ever before. He told Doris about the necklace, that it was a gift from him. It was a relief and I felt that, through what Doris communicated from Mikael, I got a wonderful confirmation and validation of the things I had experienced together with Mikael. It was like a conversation between three people. I felt more confident and felt how much this helped me living on Earth, to incorporate this new, rich inner life.

During the session, my soul brother L was also present and spoke through Doris. He wished to confirm my spiritual journey and said, that living through all of these difficulties had made me mature. He transmitted a strong and unconditional love for me. Our conversation made me understand, even better, the purpose of my life path as well as the link that exists between him, Mikael and me.

We are all part of a greater network in an infinite cosmos. When we choose to follow our soul's desire and thereby focus, summon, and listen inwards, we have the possibility to be shown glimpses of this greater network. For most of us who have chosen this path, we are amazed by how everything is connected, and that which is called chance actually is no coincidence. Instead, a pattern of interconnections emerges. They have been there through millennia, but may not have been given a prominent place in our modern society as in cultures that lived closer to nature.

Everything becomes possible when we release the constraints of what we call time and space. At the same time, we rely on our world of time and space for our development. The key is the *cooperation* between the dimensions. The vitality in our physical dimension regarding the drive for survival, sexuality, setting boundaries, and power is the Earth's contribution in this cooperation. Dimensions of unconditional love provide the necessary wise guides for these forces, which would otherwise risk being led by mere intellect without a loving inner compass. Our planet is in crisis because we have created technology that can destroy us as the wisdom to handle it is yet to be developed. It is like giving a lethal toy to an unruly child.

Love is the key to remedy this, and love is what binds all dimensions in the universe together. When earthly love and universal love meet, all is healed. To us humans, it is about initially allowing ourselves to receive this unconditional, universal love. It sounds simple but takes courage. Unconditional love sweeps everything in its path. We must surrender to forces beyond the need for control of survival. As if we could control life itself??? Life is so much greater than our intellects possibly can imagine.

To me, my three journeys to Tibet, the Andes and Egypt, were an opportunity to deepen my understanding and to be able to place my spiritual journey in a greater context. As early as 2009 I felt summoned to undertake these journeys, which were spiritually led by Marina, another clairvoyant friend. I travelled to Tibet in 2011 and had planned the journey to Peru and Bolivia long before Mikael died. As usually is the case with inner guidance, I did not initially see or understand the whole picture, instead it unravelled with time. When I was in Tibet I realised that I was partaking in Mikael's spiritual tradition – I had wished that he would have been able to travel with me, but back then he did not have the energy to manage.

It was not until the trip to Peru and Bolivia that I understood the full purpose of my journey to Tibet. Both Mikael's and my spiritual tradition were to be united energy-wise in my physical body. Later on a journey to Egypt was to come.

From the very beginning of the South American trip, I felt Mikael very strongly during the journey, which made me feel happy and joyful. Feelings of the loss of Mikael's physical presence are eased when the power in the present moment is very strong. I now know that he is happy where he is, but also happy to be together with me in this, our new life. We are now in a phase which represents a completely new life, all the way to the core and out.

The journey to South America lasted for the whole month of October 2012, starting in Peru and continuing to Bolivia. We visited several powerful places from ancient times. These are connected to a cosmological version of history, different from traditional history. This way of regarding the world creates a connection and a greater sense of belonging that fascinates me and gives my life meaning. This meaning is reinforced by concretely experiencing powerful energies at several of these sites.

For my part, the energy level and my understanding were built up gradually through different places and events to culminate when we were on La Isla del Sol (The Island of the Sun) in Lake Titicaca. Without knowing why, this place has always been a magnet to me. My inner guidance knew. It was a big step living for a month together with other people after having kept my inner life to myself for a long time. Still, at this time, we are many who are opening ourselves to a multidimensional life. And the power of the group is strong and strengthens the connection to other realms.

Everything comes together to a point in the heart. This is how Marina described her experience while we were meditating by the red pyramids, right at the start of the trip to Peru. During this meditation, I felt the energies flowing, entering through my crown chakra to continue down through the light column along my spine. My heart expanded even more. From my inner soul-meetings with Mikael, this was a familiar experience.

When I walked back from the pyramids I felt a powerful pressure over my chest, it felt like I was in a bubble. I received pieces of information about my life purpose — examining and spreading wisdom about the man-woman relationship between dimensions. Sexuality and creativity are expressed differently at higher frequencies, in which Earth needs Heaven and Heaven needs Earth.

The next meditation happened to take place on the anniversary of my soul brother's passing to the Other Side, which suited the theme for the meditation well. It brought into manifestation how everything and everyone comes together in what is termed a "Stargate". I view this "Stargate" as a place where the realms meet, and believe we create this place through joined intentions. In the state of consciousness that arises, we can more easily access the timeless dimensions.

Everyone had their own experience during the session. Many felt it as a homecoming, which was also the case for me. I found Mikael and my spiritual brother L. The three of us met in joy and confirmed our common life plan. Then the images in my mind's eye shifted: Mikael and I stood side-by-side closer to Earth while L went upwards in frequency and came closer to the light. We thanked him for all that he has given us and all that we have shared throughout our years together.

Mikael and I have our continued work closer to Earth since he has chosen to unite with me in my physical body. I also felt the connection to Kuthumi's school, which all three of us are a part of as well.

A couple of days later we flew in a small plane over the so-called Nazca lines. I was amazed with these huge prehistoric drawings that can only be seen from above. How did they do it? L was very present to me, as I saw him in the younger of the two pilots. The atmosphere reminded me of a flight we took many years ago when we flew over the Alps in a small plane. At that time L was the pilot. During the flight over the Nazca lines, universal love flowed into my body, first over my right breast through L and his connection to Kuthumi, and then over my left breast from Mikael and his long experience of the Himalayas. Everything became united in the same way I felt after Mikael's death. Back then I saw through my inner eye two hearts that melted together into one. It happened in another dimension, which now exists in my physical body. Now, in the plane in South America, the same process occurred, but this time between energies from the two traditions that we represent, between the Himalayas and the Andes.

I was completely overwhelmed. I sat by myself for a long while after the plane had landed. Within me, I spoke with Mikael. We were together very closely, and I felt both of our consciousnesses had been raised, allowing an even deeper understanding. It was a blessing that the bus ride back was long. The area above my breasts was extremely sensitive.

The morning afterwards I awoke in the most wonderful energies. Again, everything was brought together and Mikael was close to me during this. I invited him in with great joy, and he returned more deeply. *We meet like this now…* I heard him say while my light-hands were held over the thymus gland above the chest.

The journey continued and we travelled in the land of the Incas. The group became a separate energy field where every one of us kept an aspect of the whole. The atmosphere was loving and it was as if the green mountains embraced us. In the midst of the present moment, aeons of time were collected. It is a very special feeling. Trekking on the Machu Picchu mountain was a magical experience, so unendingly beautiful. To me, it was a continuation of my inner soul-meetings with Mikael. Energies from the innermost core of the Earth to the highest perspective of the Galaxies were aligned within my physical body.

Inside of me, Mikael's and my energies are being joined further and especially at the area over the thymus and the base of my throat. It feels like this is related to spreading and expressing our common message. During these soul-meetings, an energy triangle is formed between the crown chakra, the base of the throat and the thymus/heart. Our shared golden heart, forged from us both and through earthly and heavenly love, has been enriched by higher energies and ascended even higher. I can feel the joy!

My aspect in the group is as the heart's, that is to be an aspect of unconditional love. In turn, I was given this gift through my union with Mikael. I find uses for this aspect of myself and understand that this is a kind of training for me. To me, this became especially obvious at certain places we visit during the journey, and after such visits my physical longing for Mikael got particularly strong. He was so close to me in spirit. With full force, our entire physical life together welled up inside me and with it, the understanding that during all our lives together we have, and still are, each other's guardian soul. I can sense how everything is linked and that we will be together again at some point on the Other Side. But first, we need to create our new life with me here on Earth and with everything that this entails.

The morning after, Mikael came to me in partly new ways. It started with a clear beam of energy through my crown chakra, joining at the thymus. He led me through my left hand which gave healing to the right side of my body. I was touched by being given this still and gentle love to my right side. Especially the area over the breast and towards the base of my throat on the right side were affected. It was very intense and almost as much as I was able to receive. I landed in peaceful and happy company with him. At the same time, we were all the more calibrated. I felt that Mikael, from this point on, was giving from an even higher level of consciousness.

I learnt about the phenomenon, which I call "my light-hands", very early on my soul path, when I, during an inner journey, met a light-being who touched my forehead and both my hands. That night my hands were vibrating and I was filled with a powerful energy that I understood I would use in some way in the future. When I am in a meditative state or, as I call it, in an energy bubble, my hands become "light-hands" and live their own life quite beyond my conscious control. In this fashion, both I and others have been able to benefit from the energy that flows through my hands. My hands, forehead and crown build a link to the universal love that flows in my light column. It is, of course, a wonderful asset. Still, it demands a lot of my physical body. When the flow has started it is like a spring river that carries away all the debris along its path. Naturally, it is I who have attracted and agreed to this energy flow. Once I say yes to things, I need to surrender. When I struggle, it is for earthly reasons. Then I get aches and pains, or become extremely tired. I learn this again and again and return to the energy flow. When I do this, the energy pours forth in waves.

92

Towards the end of the trip to Peru, our group had the opportunity to feel the different energies at three prehistoric sites. It was as if myths that I had heard sprang to life. The people in those prehistoric times had a strong connection to the stars and different constellations. The sites that were built many thousands of years ago reflect this connection energy-wise.

The meditation at the Temple of the Pleiades was particularly memorable to me. There we sat in a circle in a kind of booth, built from large stones, which allowed us to be undisturbed during the meditation. This suited me, since it was an intense inner soul-meeting with Mikael. High energies entered my crown chakra and found me as a woman. My whole body vibrated and my tummy expanded with energy. I felt our shared connection to these ancient energies from the Pleiades. My throat chakra was expanded and at the same time, we created together. Male-female energy and sexuality in higher frequencies. My body became a vessel for these energies with the purpose of communicating the creativity, joy and pleasure in an ever more refined form.

The next day we were approaching Bolivia and Lake Titicaca, which for me was the climax of the entire journey. Our first meeting with Lake Titicaca was in a red hotel right by the shore of the lake. It felt strange to be there. It was like being on a boat as if the whole floor was unsteady. It is said that this hotel is built on top of crystals. Never before have I so clearly experienced the feeling of being on board some kind of "space-ship", or as if in a bubble of energy.

The feeling of being on board this "ship" was enhanced when the whole group meditated there. The message was that a new era is approaching bringing love and peace that will influence our Earth step by step. I found myself filled with the mild blue Christ energies and in the proximity of Lake Titicaca, I received preparations and blessings. These preparations continued as an interaction between outer places of power and my inner life. In the Andean culture, Pachamama, her womb and bosom have a particular meaning. She is both the Earth itself as a living being and the origin of everything that is feminine. In response to my resonance with these forces, I heard Mikael say: *Even I am preparing myself – as a man.* I felt so close to him and so infinitely loved.

At last, we were on Isla del Sol in Lake Titicaca. We arrived by boat and were met by my friends Justo and Lina and their young daughter Wayra. They had travelled there separately and would now continue with us for the rest of the journey. We went by foot to our hotel at the top of the hill, which had a magnificent view over the lake. The place was chosen with great care, we would be living for a few days in the heart of Titicaca.

Justo had met Mikael while he was alive, and he had helped me many years ago to find my "flower", which is another way of referring to the event that other traditions call "the inner wedding". That is to say, the meeting of man and woman within me, and in multiple dimensions. I believe it is my earlier experience of this, which makes it possible for Mikael and me to now experience and evolve together, even after his physical death. To this background, it was important for me to have a session with Justo so that I could find out about his impression of the relationship between Mikael and me at this time.

In his dream, Justo had met Mikael in the appearance of an orange coloured being, who came floating over the water and waved to him. We spoke about this and he asked me to find a flower in the same colour. During the session, Justo saw Mikael and me standing on a bridge. He described how Mikael was happy every time I built a bridge over to him. He saw Mikael's energies merging with mine.

The day after I was awakened before the alarm clock went off, by beams of sunlight shining into my room. I threw on some shawls and cardigans and went outside. I sat for an hour in the wonderfully, beautiful sunrise, letting the rays of the sun warm me. This moment developed into a loving and very close soul-meeting with Mikael.

That same day we went by boat to another part of Isla del Sol. It was a special trip. Once again we had to walk, this time to an ancient temple. The meditation we had there on a rise by the temple was a new experience for me. As it happened, I became one of four people that held the energy for the group. And I had powerful inner assistance.

I could feel how a strong wave went through me. On my left, I felt Mikael at the same level as me and on my right a little higher up, my soul brother L. Together we held the energy of unconditional love. It flowed through me and was directed towards the group. From this experience, I understood how the three of us should collaborate and what our mission in the bigger scheme is. I felt joy and fulfilment at this and naturally a greater sense of purpose and security for the future.

After this, we performed a cleansing at a spring that Justo brought us to and directly afterwards we had the opportunity to lie on a stone where women had birthed their children in days gone by. Within the group, there were several experiences of giving birth. I made a connection between the feeling of being pregnant with what is about to happen in the new era. Before I fell asleep that evening I took one last peek at a small sculpture of a man and a woman that I had bought as a souvenir that day. It stood beside the orange flower.

The next morning, I was once again awakened by golden rays of sunlight that found their way in through the window. It felt rocky as if I was on a boat.

A voice said:

— *You are in a spaceship with your two friends. Do not forget you are there. By all means, go out and meditate but remember that you are in the ship with these two.*

I covered myself with shawls and blankets and sat on a spot where I could have a view over the whole of Lake Titicaca. The sun had risen and warmed me pleasantly. The voice continued:

— *Be aware that you are in the spaceship with your friends. Yesterday you demonstrated what you can contribute as a team. Because you are three you are very powerful. You are chosen as the woman in this, due to your long training, your big heart and since you have reconciled with everything in your Earthly existence. Together with Mikael, you have shown what is possible in love between a man and a woman, through surrendering yourself in all aspects. You could take on L as a guide through your trust and love to him as a brother in the spiritual realm as well as through your long time together on Earth as co-creators. All three of you have shown unconditional love. Mikael allowed your development through your love for L and Master Kuthumi. He was there as a guardian spirit keeping the energy from his Tibetan tradition. When Mikael passed, L held the energy for both of you to unite your earthly man-woman relationship with your souls' union. L has been with you in this until this day. You demonstrate through your teamwork that the power of the group is enormous. What you have taken part of in pairs, with the third as "holder of energy" can now be united into complete oneness.*

You stand now before your Masters to receive blessings and guidance on how you can best contribute with your team. Your Masters are both women and men. We are entering a time when the female aspect will be expressed on Earth.

That is why Barbro is still there as a channel with Mikael to her left and L to her right. Together you are a mighty force.

You have practised unconditional love in all dimensions and you understand much of the power of the group. That is why you are suitable to spread this on Earth. You will know when and how, like yesterday. Mikael and L will guide Barbro from their greater perspective. Barbro will convert these impulses into practical actions. The power you three hold together is the key. You have the blessing of Heaven and Earth. Go out and speak with one voice. It is time to speak now!

I/we thanked our masters. I heard myself say yes three times and heard Mikael and L say yes three times. We thanked each other for everything we had shared together in the physical world, those experiences have made it possible for us to continue as one in this new constellation. Towards the end, when we left the ship, I had a vision of Mikael standing physically beside me to the left and L physically to my right.

Shaken, I went inside and lay on the bed. The gift I had received was overwhelming. Everything took place right after the sun rose. When I got back to my room and started writing it was no more than seven o'clock. The energies continued when I had finished writing and Mikael and I became even closer together. The bigger scheme was now quite clear allowing our roles to come to fruition. For a long time after this had happened, I was shaking. It was like everything was to be grounded in my physical body, like bringing down everything that had happened at the energy level. "Conceive in all dimensions" – that was what I had longed for and now it had just happened before me and with its climax at the Lake Titicaca. Darling Mikael!!

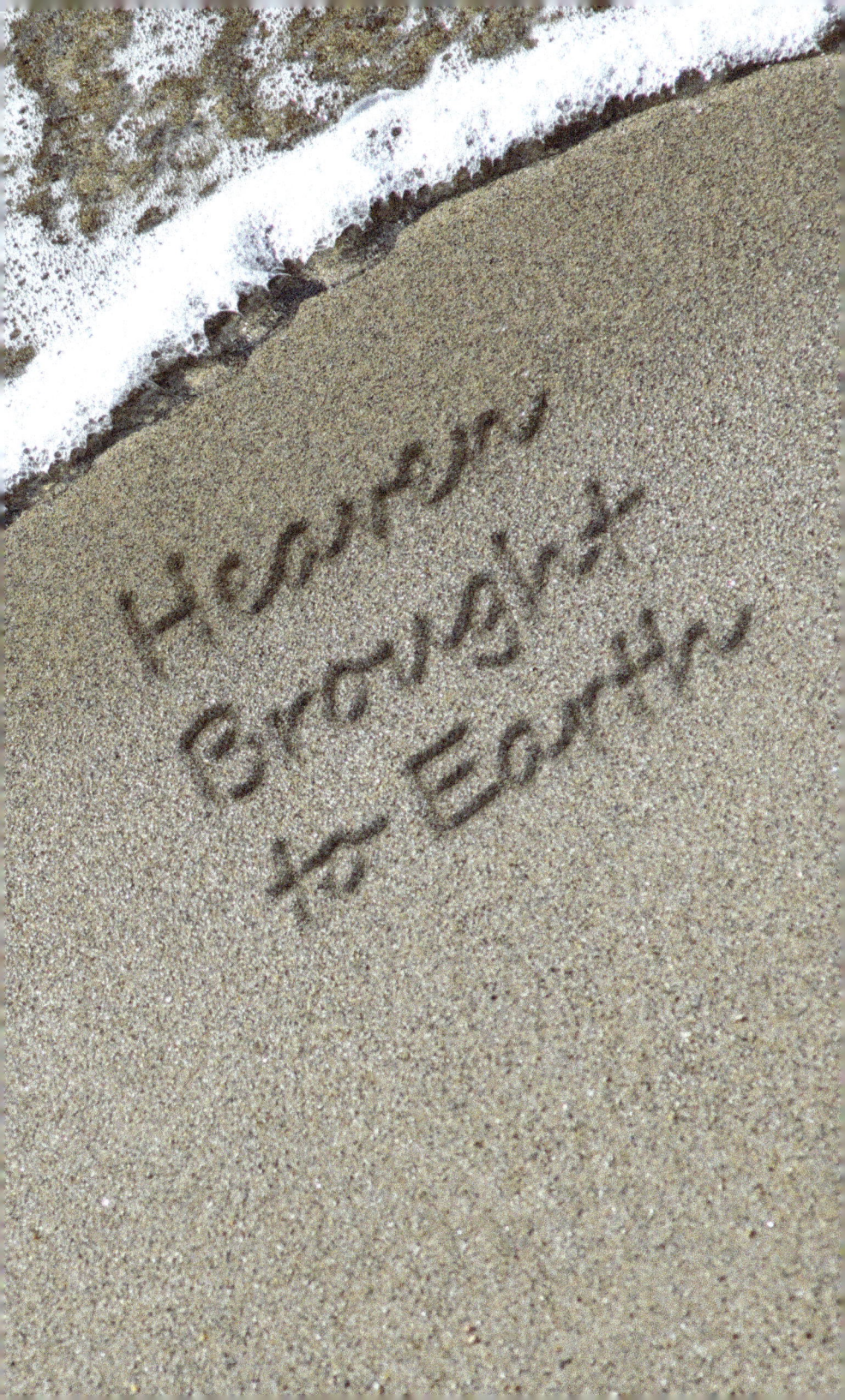

After the trip in the autumn of 2012 I find myself in a wide spectrum, with the outer physical world at one end and my all so rich inner world at the other. The stretch between these two extremes are more or less difficult to deal with, and it comes and goes in waves. Now and then I lose my way, just to be lifted up again to find the energy for dealing with both my everyday life and the building of a completely new life. At times the contrast feels painful, and at other times it feels like healing. It's all about states of consciousness. I get clear images that 2016 will be a special year when this new life will be shaped. I am getting there, step by step.

There are challenges in my surroundings. Recession and big changes in society have for the consulting business in just a few years rewritten the rules. It has become a new world which I do not recognise and where I no longer feel at home. Tasks and duties seem to tire me and I can't find my normal enthusiasm for my work. I start to realise that it is time to hand over the reins. I need to be allowed more space to follow my innermost desire, to be free to fly…

During the autumn, I look at a few places I could imagine living after Mikael's and my house has been sold, but realise that I should not tie myself down before the sale has been completed. All the same, it has been of value to imagine living in a new place and realising that I will be able to create a good life there too. Along the way I get help from the inside in the most tangible ways.

Mikael's and my inner love-life has deepened since visiting Lake Titicaca and is tender and passionate. Mikael is taking over all the more, just as I am surrendering myself all the more, something that becomes even more clear when we are undisturbed at home. I am so happy about the power and passion with which he comes to me, and he also knows how happy I am to feel him close. We have been given an unusual gift, and in time our experiences will provide joy and comfort to others, but for now it will remain a private part of our lives.

In the midst of all, I held a lecture with the theme "Spirituality in the Workplace", which was planned long before Mikael died. During the lecture, I was surrounded by my grief for him, but at the same time acknowledging that this is how it needed to be at this stage. A couple of days later I was once again caught off guard by my grief. I had been in Stockholm city, feeling like a stranger there, like a guest in that reality. On my way home, I felt crippled and as if in a vacuum. Later, when I got home and let go, grief overcame me. The deep sadness was connected to missing Mikael's and my day-to-day life together. This is the most difficult part to cope with.

In the end I went to bed, laying there just resting. Straight away Mikael came through my crown, heart and light column behind my womb. Later in the evening our soul-meetings continued, but there was a new angle to it this time. My throat chakra was opened even more than before and connected to the root chakra. Waves passed through my whole body through the light column. At another point, pent-up energy was released and I heard myself toning in higher and higher octaves. At the same time, my inner state ascended to new higher levels. At this platform Mikael and I met tenderly, peacefully and gently.

The day after was All Saints Day. I had come to realise that I needed to take care of my social grounding too, when living through my grief for Mikael. It felt important to tie our lives together at the soul level with the physical world I also live in. So, I decided to go to church that day. In the morning, I awoke to shivering high energies, which I happily greeted and enjoyed.

The morning's experience was with me when I sat in church and was able to share the physical sorrow with the others who also mourned their loved ones. I heard Mikael's name being called amongst those that had died during this year. We were treated to beautiful singing and good words, intended to give hope for a connection between the realms. I am so grateful that this connection is already there for me, so strong and full of love.

The following Sunday and for the first time since Mikael died, I made my way to the Memorial Park with its little chapel. Earlier that morning I had found two cuttings of Rhododendron in our garden and I brought them with me. They already had quite large buds. The Memorial Park is situated so beautifully by the water where small boats pass by, reminding us that life goes on. All while we who visit are near the ashes of our loved ones.

Everything came together within me, Mikael's ashes, the nature and the cuttings from our garden. I felt Mikael's presence within and how much he likes this beautiful, peaceful place. His parents' ashes lay there as well, and when my time comes, I want my ashes there too.

The chapel with its beautiful glass doors facing the sea was open. Inside were candles that could be lit. I lit three candles this time to mark a new step. One candle for Mikael, one for L and one for my old physical life. All three do not exist any longer, even if I am here in my physical body. I have left the ordinary earthly life and am entering a completely new life with a new foundation. For me this ceremony was like a near-death experience, with all that it entails.

I sat in the chapel for a long while and connected me (us) to the Divine Plan. I thanked our Masters that have gone ahead, gave thanks for our blessing and our life purpose. And I prayed for guidance on how we should best contribute and act. I realised that I had been lifted above the feelings and frequency of separation. All was healed and a new platform to live and work from had been created.

The weekend after the visit to the Memorial Park, I enjoyed a peaceful Sunday morning. A new calmness had come over me since my visit there. Mikael's dust is now revived both in our inner union and in me. This gave me a new energy to go about my day-to-day business and I could find glimpses of hope in being able to create a new life for me.

Now after breakfast, the area above the heart and towards my throat was lifted. My "light-hands" found their different places for light touches. I stood a while in the veranda door and felt how the carriage of my body was different. It reminded me of the feeling I had at the mountain Tunupa in Bolivia, during the last part of my journey there. That was the day when I was awoken at 3.30 am by an inner energy, and from my bed joined as Justo's little expedition were climbing higher up on the mountain. The feelings were very powerful. I carried myself completely differently that morning, felt completely free and with much-directed energy.

My peaceful Sunday continued and I received information from within, which I experienced as a greater and more directed power. I was told that what Mikael and I are developing through fusing our light bodies together is a new step. Through our triad with Mikael, L and me we are already ascending above the general limitations of the couple. In this frequency, we are one in the love for all of the Creation. My task here on Earth, is to transform and unite Mikael's and my physical love energy to all other energy bodies, that exist in the higher frequencies.

Later that afternoon I sat down on one of the sofas in the living room and read but I kept being interrupted. In the corner of my right eye, I saw the shadow of a man that I could identify as Mikael. I was startled and at the same time overjoyed. The veil between the realms was very thin as Mikael's presence stayed there in the other sofa. I welcomed him and raised my glass in a toast. We were there in each other's company, just like in the old days. Right before this happened, I had taken out photos of Mikael and put them on the desk and the piano. I wanted to have different pictures of him and us together, so that I didn't got stuck with a few old images. When viewing the pictures, I felt balanced. All old things had been processed now, including issues in our physical relationship, that in the past had made things difficult for us.

I understood then that our daily life had been joined to all other dimensions. Still, I was constantly reminded of how horribly hard it has been to deal with the loss of Mikael's physical presence. That is probably why Mikael appeared so clearly and was so present that we even could raise our glasses to each other from our respective sofas. At the same time, I feel that Mikael is glad that I can see a future for me here on Earth and that I am able to imagine myself in a new physical home.

I have found that in difficult times certain books are good guides. One such a book is *The Nine Eyes of Light* by Padma Aon Prakasha, which has given me great assurance. I can recognise myself in the prose of this book and I find words of understanding for what I am experiencing, which otherwise is difficult to speak to others about. Through this book, I gain perspective on my soul's path. In Egyptian mythology, my inner journey before Mikael's death, would be called "the way of Horus", which means you will develop by merging with the aura of an Ascended Master. In different ways, many of us can simultaneously and consciously access such a huge and loving aura, as we, all over the world, pray to Buddha, Jesus and so on.

What Mikael and I have been given, the gift of developing together, is termed the "Magical path of Isis", in Egyptian mythology. It is about the union of man and woman, initially on the physical level and then escalating to ever higher dimensions where we ultimately are united with the Universal Love Energy. This path has been made easier for Mikael and me, as I have already trodden the way of Horus and therefore have more easily been able to follow Mikael in his passing to the Other Side. Now he is in these higher frequencies and can in turn help me raise my energies, even though I am still here on Earth.

Mikael and I are at the beginning of a path where we ultimately will unite our souls together with the Universal Love Energy, which encompasses everything and everybody. It takes place in different steps. What happened at Lake Titicaca was a decisive step. There was the experience of the creation in energy of two golden embryos. One of them was created at Lake Titicaca, the other soon after I got home.

The autumn continued like this, with an inner life that gave me an even greater sense of wonder, while, at the same time, I met ever greater challenges in the outer world. Sometimes help arrives from unexpected places. On one of these occasions I "happened to watch" a film about twins and how close they are when one of them dies. At one level, I could directly relate. Mikael and I were each other's guardian souls, something I feel very strongly. Several sources have spontaneously and independently confirmed that.

I am also strongly connected to my soul brother L but in a different way. It feels like we have had many lives together. Some think that there are different forms of twin souls, I'm not sure. When L died, to me it was like when Tage, from the Swedish comedian duo *Hasse & Tage*[8], died prematurely. Through their humour they transformed Swedish society. This duo was a creative twosome like L and me. When L. died I felt diminished in my professional life. I had lost my playmate with whom I had built up so much.

Mikael is my *husband*, my other half of man-woman on the Other Side. With everything that has happened since his death, I understand that I am eternally his cosmic woman. It feels as we are the same creature, same soul, and I feel half without him on my existential platform. The film gave me understanding and thereby calm. Our gift and our contribution is to meet up in this strong love relationship between worlds. We are elevated to a high energy level that would not be possible with both of us on Earth.

The day after watching the film, I found a great photo of Mikael that I have had in my purse for many years. It was taken sometime during our first months together, and even though it was quite crumpled, it still portrayed a happy and naked Mikael. I remember that he described himself as my "lover boy". To me he was a real good-looker and he knew it. We made love often and passionately...

Last weekend I was given a nice drawing by our grandchild who is six years old. It shows two people with a heart on each and a large heart in between. They are holding each other's hands and are sort of forced away from each other. In a child's way, he shows what is happening as he sees and senses a lot. A few days later I was

---

8) *Hasse & Tage* (Swedish: *Hasse och Tage*) was the popular Swedish comedy duo featuring Hans "Hasse" Alfredson and Tage Danielsson. They are sometimes known as *Hasseåtage*, a name created by the Swedish press in the 1960s, but never used by the duo themselves. (https://en.wikipedia.org/wiki/Hasse_%26_Tage)

told that the picture represented how Mikael "jumped" to Barbro, and that is just how it is, when Mikael comes to me as a strong energy. Children know...

In the midst of this unsettled period I am supported from within by Mikael. And yet I need to ask for his help in order to connect. If I lose myself in anxiety or sorrow, I break the connection that to me is like a vital nerve. One morning I awoke at around five am as anxiety was creeping up on me. These feelings were hard to stop at first, but when I finally prayed my prayer as usual and asked for help to raise myself over the sorrow and anxiety, I immediately felt calmer.

I understood from within that if I don't stay in love and peace, I will hinder our inner triumvirate from being able to work in its strongest way. After a while I became more and more free and fell back to sleep after making a few practical decisions, amongst which to leave my role as managing director at the consulting company where I work.

A couple of hours later I woke up to these words from Mikael: *I have come close to you. We are united, never forget!* At the same time, I experienced a high sensitivity in my body. When I asked for, and received help to stop the crippling sorrow that lower my frequency, Mikael could come through strongly.

I learnt to look at business differently. As a group, we ourselves at the consulting firm, need to live the change we wish for society. That is our greatest task before making money, even if it means just surviving as a business. Survival energy inhibits creativity. This is something I strongly believe in, have written about as well as lectured on. Now it is about us and our ability to stay in the flow beyond survival.

Later that evening Mikael came back. I was lying on the sofa and had "disappeared" after my little tea time. It was like I was in a cocoon surrounded by energies. Just like in the morning my body became charged and hypersensitive. *I arrived like this in the morning and I am here like this now too!* I heard Mikael say. All my cells were vibrating. "I will never again doubt that our union is real," I replied. "My beloved lover!"

He's not coming back, that is to say to our day-to-day existence here at home. I had heard these words and then repeated them to myself the whole day before this deliverance took place and the flow was released. In the depth of me, I needed to accept this fact and allow myself to grieve, otherwise I would get stuck in sorrow. After this event, the incapacity was released. I could embrace the sorrow and infuse it with light and love.

In the middle of December 2012 my physical platform had begun to stabilise. Something has released in my gut and been replaced by a warmth, which to me felt like it is connected to an ancient sense of abandonment and loneliness. Through our love, Mikael and I had cured each other's loneliness, but it returned for me when he died. I sense how many lonely hours he had at home, while I was out and flew around working. Now, when I think back on this, I believe I was afraid he would die. I didn't want to be apart from him but I needed the time and space to receive and learn from the energies. It was wise. It turned out as a prerequisite for the steps to come.

As the "Days of Light" retreat is approaching, I feel strongly that I need to spend time with likeminded friends this special time before Christmas. Especially with those who can understand some of what Mikael and I are experiencing. Many of us are awakening to contact with other worlds and I feel how good it will be to meet others with this common focus.

All around the world and amongst people like me, who wish to follow their soul's desire in a way that is freer than traditional religion, 21st of December 2012 has been hailed as a great paradigm shift. I have rather thought or felt that we humans are part of something so great that we cannot comprehend with our normal brains. Just as we physically experience nature's cycles and those in our human lives, I imagine that we are part of even greater and more far-reaching cosmic cycles. I cannot express in words how this greater pattern is constructed or what it encompasses, but I can intuitively feel the correlations.

Whatever this transition is about, the build-up is bringing about a huge focus of energies. It is apparent that there are many of us who are longing for and experiencing many other dimensions while living here on Earth. Speculations about the date have for some taken on proportions that feels very remote to me. It touches everything from doomsday prophecies to dreams of a wholly loving world in one instant. I don't believe that we humans would cope with such drastic change. I believe we would break. I imagine that we in this transition will be able to receive particularly high and loving energies. Whether we can receive these is up to each and every one of us. Receiving love is not so simple, even if most of us long for it. I believe that we need to come together and support each other.

It is in light of this that I decided to attend the "Days of Light" retreat taking place three days before Christmas 2012. I have known the organiser of these days since the beginning of the '80s, which means I have long-standing confidence in her. She is the same person with whom I journeyed to the Amazon, Tibet and Peru/Bolivia. During the festival, those who felt summoned gathered and worked through guided meditations, channelled from the spiritual world.

The information I receive during these meditations hit right home and agree well with my focus. It mirrors perfectly the struggles I experienced in my day-to-day life regarding my grief for Mikael, but also how necessary it is to embrace this grief without getting stuck in it. I remember how crucial this insight was, as I heard myself both think and several times say: *He's not coming back*, that is to say, not physically back into my life again. However, it does take time to accept this fully.

At the retreat, I am helped to raise myself over my physical sorrows, to allow them to exist but not linger. The feeling I have is that everything is possible, that everything can be created. I need to be available for what will happen, to love all the cells of my body. I am so grateful to be receiving this kind of love so strongly through my inner union with Mikael.

The high-point of the retreat was for most of us the end of the second day. To me, the earlier meditations had been quite physical. The first evening I was totally wiped out and went to bed early. The morning of the second day I felt a new kind of energy enter my head. It then moved down to my heart via the area behind my navel and womb and turned into vibration and heat in these areas. On the afternoon of the second day I saw colours in my mind's eye. To my surprise it was a yellow egg with crystalline shapes inside, that was in an otherwise completely white field that I experienced as having several layers.

I could not express in words what I had experienced, more than it was related to receiving the so-called "crystal energy" in this concrete form. During the meditation, we were guided to receive a gift from a "crystal angel". I then received this egg that I had already seen. In the next part of the meditation we were encouraged to share from the gift we had received. I saw this egg which took on different colours, spreading parts of itself as in a dance. It reminded me a lot of some of the pictures I had seen on Mikael's computer before the summer. During the retreat I have a feeling of the entirety like a mosaic where every piece contributes to the whole. The power of the group is tangible. Together we are elevated in energy. We return home afterwards with this inspiration to support us on our continued paths.

Then came Christmas Eve, my first Christmas celebration without Mikael physically with me. After all that I had received during the Days of Light festival, I was not feeling the loss as strongly, as I was rather filled from the inside. Also, at home I felt his presence so strongly. I also felt strongly how the yellow "crystal egg" was carried within me as a gift. To me, it has become a symbol of Mikael's and my union in a dimension of completeness, universal love and light. I don't know why it is called "crystal energy", but I and many others perceive it as Christ energy. That is, the energy that cuts through the darkest shadows with its powerful gentleness. This energy enables ut to ascent to ever higher levels together. I went to the Christmas prayer ceremony at church with this passion and presence within me. This will be a new tradition in my new life.

On Christmas Day the entire family got together for the last time in Mikael's and my house. Everybody wanted to cherish this moment, knowing that the house would soon be sold. It was a glorious family get-together and our youngest grandchild stayed over until Boxing Day. Mikael felt very present to all of us.

In the morning before the family arrived and I was alone, I sat in the sofa and brought in Mikael's soul before meeting everybody. High energies started to flow and I lay down to receive them. Especially the upper chest, throat and jaws were activated. My left hand was, as always in our soul-meetings, Mikael's spokesperson. This occurs quite beyond my thought as if the hand has a life of its own. At this time, it gently caressed my cheeks and chin. The love from Mikael flowed straight into me and spread throughout my body. Tears of love and joy came. Then Mikael's voice came from the left: *I thank you, Barbro!*

This "thank you" made my whole body relax. It meant so much. It encompasses all that we had been through together since Mikael passed over, the fact that I am still here on Earth uniting the dimensions. Our large family was also present in this thanking.

Beloved Mikael! What we experience is a wonder, a miracle! I gladly receive your gratitude for my part in all this. It gives my life here on Earth purpose. You know my gratitude for you, that you held the energy while I received inner teaching and preparation through L. My thanks also to you for, after your passing, choosing to be with me in our union. Your thanks soothe me. It helps me through the earthly longings.

The night after Boxing Day was very intense. I was awakened in the middle of the night by a transfer of high energies that affected old tensions in my left leg from the groin and down. It was connected to the left cheek where I had a bridge removed from a tooth. The day before it had started to ache around the screws beneath where the bridge had been. I thought an inflammation was about to arise there and had resigned myself to a visit to the dentist.

The following days and nights the high energies continued to pass through my body. These old tensions that had come back, became transformed to warmth and heat in my body. There was no longer any trace of the inflammation that had been about to arise in my jaw. Everything became more peaceful and clear. I felt as if my experience of space-time had been altered. I was emptied of thought and could without difficulties be in the empty space, the place which is the root of inspiration. It helped that I was at home and not working during this time. I felt strongly that we were about to enter a new era, but what it would entail was at that time unknown to us all, which I felt was all right. All one needs to do is just following the flow.

My inner soul-meetings with Mikael showed me mysteries that aroused a sense of wonder which was almost more than I could cope with in my physical existence. My experiences however, were so concrete and tangible that I couldn't help but accept them. I choose just to receive this gift. The most important thing, I thought, is what they lead to. Through all of this I have received a love that is beyond all I thought was possible. That makes me light, free and happy despite the fact that I still often miss my beloved husband physically. "You know him by his fruits", is a quote from the Bible. These lines have been a help in discerning and daring to trust those experiences that are beyond the logic of the intellect. I also believe that what I am going through is equipping me to better contribute constructively to this world.

Few books describe what I am experiencing, but there are some and I use them. One of these books is written by Padma Aon Prakasha with the title "Womb Wisdom". It describes the feminine path to spiritual wisdom, a path that is so much more physical than inner spiritual journeys often are made out to be. It describes love life in connection to higher dimensions. When I read it, it gave me a sense of meaning and understanding. When reading it my womb would begin vibrating, all the way from the area behind my navel and up towards the heart and a warmth spread out from that region.

It really felt like incubating an egg or an embryo that is a merger of Mikael's and my souls in a higher dimension. What I have read and heard from other spiritual sources is that we "give birth" to ourselves into ever higher dimensions. Back then, when first reading about this, I didn't know how that actually happens. Perhaps some people experience this visually, as images in the mind's eye, while I experience it mostly bodily? Additionally there was this strong feeling of Mikael's and my light bodies as joined. This ought to mean, that in some other dimension we have the same origin. In reality, it is impossible to express in words these kinds of experiences, but the fact is that they exist, which fills many of us with wonder.

The night gave way to the morning of New Year's Eve. I had not been able to sleep. It was simply impossible to just fall back asleep after the magnitude of what I had been through. Mikael came as energy behind my womb and above. We met calmly. Calm in the pulses. It was very still but with great intensity. Before this Mikael went directly to my heart which expanded and the energy rose upwards. The energies met from each side over the chest. At the same time, it vibrated and was warm in my womb and centring around the navel area. *Celebration!*

I heard this word several times. The energies came together in celebration of the cosmic union between Mikael and me. Celebrating our union and our merger in the crystal egg.

I felt there were so many levels and aspects to what was happening. A lot to take in. No wonder it was hard to fall asleep. I soon realised I was grateful that Mikael insisted on showing the importance of me understanding this. He approached me in an earnest solemn way. Our calm energy and light meetings were transformed into tender conversations. Often, I hear or listen but this particular night Mikael's words were placed on my tongue and he spoke through me. That had happened once before, earlier in the autumn, and during a particularly intense period. Now it was time again. It was as if he wanted to help me cope with the greatness of it all.

— *All this is possible since you are still on Earth. It is only our love that makes it possible. It is a lot for you to get through. But know I am always with you. Never doubt that!*

I needed to pass over and become free to be able to love in this way. We both have our mission in this. You keep yourself young in this way. Here, where I am, everybody is young. I am so grateful. And you have known all along!

I replied that I had known some of it, but had never been able to imagine what we now are going through and that I also always believed that he too had some premonition of it.

— *True, but then I didn't want to admit it as concretely as you.*

The conversation went back and forth for long, and all the while my left hand lived its own life and caressed my cheeks and hairline tenderly. Mikael was right, as a human I really needed this tenderness. It was also obvious that I needed support and that it is allowed to sometimes feel like a small human being who is going through things far beyond normal reasoning. In these dimensions, normal physical laws cease to be applicable. I realised that it requires a lot of me when it comes to being able to live simultaneously on Earth... Very few people could understand what I was experiencing. Even in spiritual circles, it seemed to be unusual... or was it just too private?

It is now a new year, 2013. Mikael died three quarters of a year ago. It has been a time of extreme upheaval. I am not, and can never be, the same again. I have been elevated to other realms and have gained experiences that will be with me forever.

My challenge now is how to live with all of these changes and experiences in this, our day-to-day world. Clashes come one after the other and I need to handle them and decide how I want to live my life from now on. It is in many ways like living parallel lives while waiting to find ways to fully be able to live as the new person I have become.

Meeting the family is of course precious and something I really want to do, but during this time I was still fragile and needed breaks in between all social interactions. Still, family is and will always be an important anchor in my earthly life and connects the realms for me, with Mikael as a helping link on the Other Side. So much love…

During this time, when I take a break after being out and about, I allow myself to be led to one or another TV program with an inspiring theme. If I do not give enough time or space to receive the energies that are coming almost constantly, there can easily be a clash. Blocked Kundalini energy can make you feel ice-cold and frozen to the very bone. I have learnt to wrap myself up in blankets and build a cocoon and like that just receive the energies. Often the icy chill transforms to heat and the flows begin again. I have spent many nights like that.

In the new year, I also felt the need to let my new and transformed me get going professionally. At the consulting firm, I could hide my new self a little as part of a group of colleagues. This was harder when it concerned Mikael's and my shared business. How could I write on our website that my beloved husband and colleague is no longer alive? How would I find words to express my situation and what could be offered now in Mikael's and my business, *Curmans Gestalt AB*? I felt it was a necessary and big step to go out into the world in new ways. I was gently assisted by a friend and colleague who helped me step by step. To me she felt like a kind of midwife, helping me to remain faithful to myself but still expressing myself in a fashion that works on our website and publicly. My colleague is also very knowledgeable when it comes to technology, which made things much easier.

Before and after the work with the website, Mikael came very strongly to me, as if to help me through this difficult process. To me, I felt as if we were working together. Through this I learned how new creations happen, by the exchange of our energies. This rhythm of energy-work became all the more part of my everyday life. My feeling is that I have volunteered to contribute in this way. It was clear to me that this is how energetical changes come about in the world. But before experiencing it myself, I hadn't understood that it occurs so concretely and physically. It is all very tangible and the changes always begin with my everyday world.

The first days of the new year had thus been a breakthrough regarding energy. And more would happen. I felt as if my old life no longer suited who I had become, and it was clear to me that I would have to leave it behind in some way. In my private life, I needed to sell our house and find a new place to live. I felt I was not the same person professionally, and needed to deal with the consequences of that too.

I was in several ways renewed in my physical body as well. Strangely enough I also needed to renew everything from most of my kitchen appliances to my old car. It was like everything needed to be renewed.

For many years I had not felt at home or able to identify myself with my branch association. During the last decade, I had solved this by keeping a passive stance. Then, a number of events came along that made me decide to leave the association completely. I had thought about remaining passively, but I was awoken three times during one night, which made me understand that it was time to act. It was time to express my truth in public.

After considering it for a few days I wrote an article that was published on the Internet. The morning after it was published, I woke up with a chesty cough and fever. It was the flu, but for me it meant so much more. I am very seldom ill. This timing was no coincidence. Afterwards I realised that working on the website had been the start of this for me. This transformation was necessary as a basis for me going out in public in other ways. My influenza was a cleansing of my system. It felt good to sweat out the old to make room for the new.

Towards the end of those few days with the flu, Mikael came to me in an especially calm and gentle fashion, starting in my crown chakra. It transformed into a still and loving soul-meeting in my heart. My left hand held the right hand and both of them came to rest at the base of my throat. After a while I started crying, an old cry, and I became sore deep down in my throat. It was in the same place the deep cough had been, which was still there a little. It turned into inner healing. Calm, still and finally the connection was there all the way from the crown, through the throat, heart and all the other chakras. Calm and content with this, I lay there a long while and enjoyed it.

Within me L was present much more strongly than in a long time, which was natural since we shared a common platform in our working life. It was also very dear to me to feel his joy for Mikael's and my union and the collaboration between the three of us. I awoke in the morning with my arms above my head, as they so often are. I had a special feeling this time, as if I'd been out flying. I got images in my mind of us three in beautiful colours. It's the first time I've seen such clear imagery from the Other Side.

Your arms have been wings – you have been out of your body, I heard a voice say, but didn't know who. I just felt happy that the three of us had been able to meet and fly together and that I had been able to see what it looked like on the Other Side. I had longed for that opportunity. The gap between the realms is sometimes great and challenges in the outside world often block the flow.

One evening I felt heavy and thoughts about the upcoming move led me to be drawn to Mikael's and my bedroom, which had become only his for his final years, as we then slept in different rooms. Back then, the decision to have separate bedrooms had felt so hard for me to make, as I always have had a strong desire to feel his skin and warm body close to mine. How could I possibly choose to sleep in my own room? Now, in retrospect, I understand and see it as a preparation for what now has happened. The pain would have been insufferable to cope with, should he have left me while we still shared our double bed.

I sat down on a chair in the bedroom and began talking with him, at the same time allowing the tears to come. I told him how much I missed his embrace and skin. How right until the end I saw him as an attractive man and the man of my life, but that I still needed my own room to be able to cope with the energy transfers of each early morning. Because I followed that path we are able to meet each other as we do now. Another reason for me to decide to sleep in my own room the last couple of years, may also be because I at some level could perceive what would happen and hence protected myself in advance. This conversation and closeness with Mikael was a strong moment that after a while turned into a joyful and loving one.

Later that evening when I lay in bed, there was a kind of continuation of our conversation earlier in the day. I was a little cold so I wrapped myself up in my meditation blanket under the duvet. I warmed up and lay on my left side to sleep. Then something very strange happened. The energies in my back became so clear that I felt that the duvet was moving. It felt like Mikael was spooning me with his energy. We used to sleep in this position often.

The energies grew in strength over my entire back and legs. They entered my heart, which expanded and felt like it would explode. I just allowed it, let them in and said: "You can go right through me!" And so it was. My whole body was released in waves of energy.

My whole body was shaking. It came from my heart and spread downwards. I allowed and surrendered myself into a soft, strong and loving energy. I fell asleep, embedded in love. We were one in my physical body. I felt completely soft and in a way dissolved.

When I woke up in the morning after many hours of peaceful sleep, we were still there in the same energy field. I came back with the help of the blue sky, the sun and a quiet breakfast. Later that evening the soul-meetings continued. Something was going on and I lay down on the bed to rest. After a while a very powerful energy emerged from the base of my spine. My whole body shook and the energy went direct into my cells. It was an intense meeting of higher energies from above and the powerful energy in and close by the tailbone. The energy went right into my womb, the energy that I call the "crystal egg", which grew and vibrated. It was very tangible that something new was developing in that fashion and was living as an energy in my physical body.

An inner dialogue with Mikael began:

— *Remember that our soul-meetings are important. They build up the energy that you bear within you. This energy is the very basis for what will happen. It is already being transmitted wherever you are and through whatever you are doing. It is also helping you to be a light for others in the darkness that exists right now. It helps you release anxiety. So, allow yourself time so we can meet and build it up. It is not only for our pleasure, even if that is wonderful too.*

Transformation and creating a whole new life concerns both my private living and my group of consultants. Mikael's and my inner soul-meetings help me manage all this at the same time. I am vitalised and feel surrounded by love in all of it. I also understood all the more that the essence of what will become was already there in energy and that it materialises in me through our inner soul-meetings. This understanding gives purpose to my life and to me it felt, and still feels, as if I am a radio antenna, sending signals out to those who can pick them up. Together, projects and environments are built up in this way. L was of course an active partner in this. He was holding the energy for us.

In many of these soul-meetings I experienced that there was a form of downloading of energy far beyond what I could comprehend through the intellect alone. The energy that entered into me was quite electric and created a bubble of energy each time. To me, it was obvious that I should not interfere with my personality. Just let it happen.

I have learnt for many years to allow energies in this manner. Now with Mikael on the Other Side it is even more obvious that blocks and hindrances are signs of something that I have not brought to completion. When I get past such a blockage, like the time when I spoke with

Mikael in our bedroom, the gates open and energy flows with even greater power. To me it feels like water that's been pent up behind a dam. When the dam opens the water surges with even greater force to gradually calm down and adopt a calmer pace.

Another rhythm that I have been able to recognise for many years, is the rhythm between creative period of incubation that changes into a strong energy in the outside world, a kind of manifestation. The shifts in this process can be larger or smaller. The long incubation time that I experienced during the autumn and the beginning of 2013 was demanding. Vacuum is amongst the most difficult things we human beings have to experience, being there in uncertainty about what will happen.

Towards mid-February the vacuum was released and a lot began to happen both within me and on the outside. Mikael's and my home was starting to be broken up since parts of the house was being renovated before it was to be sold. Moving boxes illustrated what would soon happen in a larger scale. In all this I shift between vulnerability and sorrow on the one hand, and on the other hand a deeper understanding of the meaning. For a long time, I had felt that I lived completely different lives in the same physical existence, with transition periods in between. At this time, I found myself in such a transition period, waiting for my third life in this physical existence to enter in.

When the vacuum was released, our inner light meetings took on another character and became even more profound. Earlier, and only on special occasions, Mikael's energy had taken over and he had placed his words on my tongue. This time the same thing happened but in another way. Now there was a very gentle caressing of the skin on my right hand, which gradually became so strong that tears of joy welled up. My heart was vibrating as it was opening up all the more. At this time, also in soul, I was able to feel my skin against Mikael's skin again. Calmly, and moment by moment. In my chest, I experienced an intensity that rose towards my throat chakra. The skin and throat chakras! I would never have been able to figure this out intellectually. In hindsight, I can see the pattern though. Love opens up the throat chakra, the area which is about our ability to express to the world who we are. I understood that Mikael wanted to show me that we would also merge in the area of the throat chakra and hence be able to speak as with one voice. In the same way, we had been able to meet skin to skin, to be one there as well.

Then insight struck me like a bolt of lightning. The new life that was being formed truly was a union of both of our energies. The closeness to Mikael was complete, we were coming together as one single soul being, and this process would be completed in few years' time. These are of course mind-boggling ideas and events in the eyes of us living in the ordinary world here on Earth. Because of that, Mikael's and my experiences would have to remain private for the time being. Still, within me I knew it to be true. I felt alive and happy in the midst of the sorrow and sense of loss.

The inner soul-meetings that followed confirm my experience. I received new downloads of energy almost every day and the energies that entered my crown chakra lifted me all the higher. I understood that I also needed to accept help during this difficult period. That is to say, my first birthday without Mikael by my side and then his birthday a month later - he died two days after his birthday.

I realised how brittle I was when I interpreted a piece of information about the anniversary of Mikael's death in a way that frightened me. I thought that would mark the time when Mikael would in fact leave our union and that I would no longer be able to be together with him in soul. Something which meant so much to me, and which I had become used to ever since he passed over. That the union would still be there but that I would not be able to perceive it, while still on Earth. I thought that he had his soul journey to undertake on the Other Side and I did not want to hold him back. Apart from that we had for many years celebrated our birthdays together, often closer in time to his. I liked to take it easy on my birthday, go around anonymously in town and enjoy a good meal just him and me.

I was about to cancel the family's visit on my birthday but chose to call one of my clairvoyant friends instead. It was through that phone conversation, that I realised I had misinterpreted the message. How Mikael and I will come together in the future is up to me being able to raise myself in energy. When I become scared and full of doubt my frequency diminishes of course. I learn this same lesson again and again and it is not so strange actually, it demands a lot to be a "bare bridge" between the worlds. To live in these high frequencies but at the same time be there in an environment where most people find what I experience to be a bit odd and weird. On the other hand, I have chosen that path with pleasure.

The birthday was like balm to the soul. My grand-children helped me along in their different ways. My youngest noticed that I was not really present and won-dered why. When I told her, I missed her grandfather on my birthday she understood at once. Later on, she brought me into my bedroom and sang "Happy birthday dear grandma" to me. One of the other grandchildren had done a new drawing. This time it showed Mikael as someone flying in the centre with a smiley above, a red heart to the left and to the right a tree with two birds that chirped both "kvi-vit" and "bom-bom". "Grandpa is a spirit now," he said. And I understood both that Mikael had taken a new step on the Other Side and that I had become lost, in the same way as after the funeral. I was also given a beautiful orange rose, a colour that to me is connected to Mikael's spiritual tradition.

After this was resolved in the outer world, Mikael came to me with full force. Now I was open enough and had released the things that pulled me down in frequency. He spoke clearly to me:

— *It is time for the throat[9] now, Barbro! We shall go public together. I am with you always. We are conjoined. Never doubt this!!! What we have united during the past year is the foundation for it. Now it will be shaped in the outer world. Focus there. Higher energies to be taken in. All according to our agreement from the beginning.*

Mild, lovely energies flowed into me. Then I heard the voice again, coming from my own mouth:

— *Pleasure is not forbidden, quite the contrary. It is not about that. It is about letting go.*

After this inner soul-meeting, my entire body became very relaxed and I could enjoy a beautiful day and evening. I had my energy back again, and with ease I was able to take care of my daily tasks.

The following weeks these soul-meetings continued and I became more and more energetically open, all the

9)   In this setting is meant the throat chakra

way from my crown down to my feet. Simultaneously, I was given practical teaching followed by bodily sensations as if to illustrate what I just had been taught. It reminded me in part of the teaching I had received through my Master Kuthumi, every night for five years. Maybe it was he that continued, when a voice said:

— *Your collarbones have a decisive part to play when the throat chakra expands.*

The same information had come to me during the autumn's journey with the extra knowledge that we all have information coded within our bones, information that comes out when the time is right.

During the first days of March we planned everything that involved selling Mikael's and my home. The sons and I were together in this and it felt good. The following days Mikael took part by coming to me several times and in an intense way. A very apparent co-creation between the outer and inner. My throat chakra opened even more and connected with the whole chest. It was like a Kundalini eruption in my chest cavity and as if gates were opened the whole way through my body, and more intensely around the area behind the "crystal egg". The energies poured through both my breasts with my heart in the centre, then ascending higher and higher until the whole throat and jaw area were electrified. I surrendered completely to the flow of these very powerful energies, and the whole experience to me felt like an initiation to higher energy levels. It felt so real that I chose to drop my usual need for control and allowed to receive from this Divine source.

There are different channels through which we humans can perceive the spirit world. Some see auras around people or get strong images, others have sudden insight that become certainty and thoughts, others hear voices within them, while others experience bodily sensations. We are all different and we often have one or maybe a couple of channels that are most natural to us. I feel mostly through bodily sensations, which is the way it all began for me, but after some time I also started to hear beyond my physical ear. I have often longed to be able to 'see' more, just because these senses are strongest, and above all to be able to see how life can be on the Other Side.

One beautiful spring day, when I sat in the sun in the garden I got what I'd wished for so long. I had the opportunity to fly away with Mikael in soul and see what he showed me. Once, many years ago, I had the same opportunity with the help of my master Kuthumi, who taught me about that. *Travel with your forehead*[10]! I heard him say and at first I didn't understand what he meant. I then learned to keep my focus concentrated in the forehead and approach him that way and at the same time listen to the birds. My body felt heavy at first but I got lighter after a while, and so I got to fly with him to his retreat on the etheric plane.

Now when I sat in our garden in the spring sunshine I heard the birds and recalled my inner flight with master Kuthumi. I asked Mikael for help to fly with him and that he would show me what he wanted me to see. I took in high energies through my crown and especially through the third eye. The energies made my body feel light. Conscious that I was sitting in my chair in the sun, I allowed myself to be carried towards the birds, singing up in the air. After a while I could feel Mikael's presence to my left. We flew together, at first it was as though I needed to practice and he helped me. After that we just enjoyed each other's company as two free souls. A loving moment in a higher place.

---

10) In this setting is meant The Third Eye Chakra

133

Then we arrived in Tibet. Mikael showed me a place where he had had many incarnations, a place he loved. It was his place and his brotherhood was there in orange clothes. There was an infinite sense of peace at this place, you felt at one with nature. Mikael explained this and I understood with my entire being. Mikael hinted that there had been other lives for his soul but we did not go there.

Love is the theme for our life together. Mikael was happy to tell me this. Then I recollected the vision I was given already the year before we first met. Christ was standing on a hill and summoned me up to the white fire that was there in a sparkling dome. He just stood there and welcomed me in with his right hand. It took me a few years before I dared to. Now I invited Mikael to join me – we stood there together and bathed in this light, this fire. L arrived too and we formed our triad in that light, in the fire and reminded each other of our oaths. The three of us stood there for a long time in this, the basis for our common mission. Joy and free expectations.

It took me a while to return to my armchair in the sun. I was assisted by the sun itself and by the birds. I remember that I said joyfully to Mikael and L: "I can be in many places at the same time." That is also the way...

The following days I had the pleasure of meeting Mikael on the Other Side in even more ways. It was as if he wanted to reinforce our connection between the realms. It made me feel secure. It began one early morning around three o'clock. This "happened" to be exactly one year after Mikael went into the hospital never to come home again. Two weeks later he died there. This early morning, I was still awake after the night's intense soul-meeting and I sat down to write. Right at the moment when I sat down to start writing, something happened to the candle flame beside me on the coffee table. In the corner of my eye I saw how it flickered wildly as wanting my attention. I put down the pen and a dialogue with Mikael began, by the help of the candle flame. We conversed through the beams from the flame, which grew upwards in different shapes.

Then it became even clearer. The rays of light were now directed completely towards me like a path of light all the way to my heart and the "crystal egg". I felt the heat in my body. It was a meeting in powerful love. It was also very demanding. I needed to concentrate deeply and keep my focus in the forehead to be able to follow the rays of light. I stayed there for a while but then I lay down and fell soundly asleep. I woke up a few hours later and made my way into bed. My whole body was shivering as though I had a fever. I fell asleep and was awakened by the alarm clock. The candle that was standing on the coffee table showed clear signs that the candle flame had been pointing in my direction and horizontally. I decided to keep the candle lit for now, realising that I had been far away in another world. I remembered, when the energies were at their strongest, I was speaking another language. As if from another life. The days and nights carried on this way. The soul-meetings via the candle flame deepened when I got more used to them and wasn't as shocked as I was the first time.

Later in March I went to an exhibition of Hilma af Klint's esoteric art[11]. There were very strong images that affected me deeply. The reaction to the exhibition came afterwards at home. Flashes of light by my right temple carried on in the corner of my eye for an entire hour. All night and the day after were like being in another world. Once again, this shaking fever that later turned into heat. From the eyes and upwards I was pounding

---

11) Hilma af Klint (October 26, 1862 – October 21, 1944) was a Swedish artist and mystic whose paintings were amongst the first abstract art. A considerable body of her abstract work predates the first purely abstract compositions by Kandinsky. (https://en.wikipedia.org/wiki/Hilma_af_Klint)

and vibrating. I just tried to accept. It felt like a preparation for times to come. I cancelled some appointments that would have been too much at that time.

At the same time, step-by-step we were getting ready and closer to selling the house, and I felt I was now prepared within. I also kept getting inner images of my new place. It felt airy and light and a home where Mikael and I could live as free souls. From this new place, it felt even easier to manifest our common mission, that it would be more accessible.

The outer world and the inner world had now been joined firmly hand in hand. One morning I woke up from an influx of extremely gentle but strong energies. I was spoken to and understood that it was master Kuthumi and master Sananda with their female partners. The energy was so refined and gentle while at the same time penetrating all my chakras from top to bottom.

I had laid down in a warm blanket as if in a cocoon, which to me felt like a place where receiving from only the highest source should take place. I slept the whole night peacefully. The time was ripe and I heard:

– *You are blessed. See your worthiness in what is happening. In our time, it is the women that go out with the message (enlightenment) and with their husband within them. Earlier it was the other way around.*

I felt L so close, strongly connected to Master Kuthumi, and he in turn, infused with the love of Christ – the white light. I felt their blessing for Mikael's and my union. The blessing was for us both, but also a acknowledgement of all that we had achieved.

The day after it was time to visit the dentist. My old bridge on the lower left jaw needed to be completely removed, screws and everything. This has been a carrier of symptoms since my youth. A couple of weeks before Mikael's death the area became infected and the bridge was partly removed. It felt like a sign that the old stuff must go. The jaw needed to rest for quite some time before it was time to put in a new bridge. Again, it was time for renewal.

I got through Mikael's birthday by spending the whole day at Sturebadet, a spa in Stockholm which was founded by his great-grandfather. It feels like a symbolic act of purifying, ahead of everything new that is soon to arrive. Soon the night when he passed over arrived. Throughout that day, we had an intense contact with the help of the candle flame. It was as if we together were experiencing the reverse birth, something death de facto is. I wanted to stay awake and be there during those hours, to relive how it was a year ago. He died at 2.30 am. Just at that time I fell asleep and woke up an hour later. It was meant to be, we were close to each other in another world.

In the morning, I called my spiritual adviser Marina as we had agreed. She had a clear contact with him and told me:

– *He is waiting for you and helping you up. He has chosen to do so.*

It was good to know that my worry about pulling him down was unfounded.

– *It's not like that – everyone is being raised and you also. He passed over to be able to contribute in this very special event. He is helping you and says that you must be on Earth with the people to contribute. It is a collaboration between the realms.*

A quarter of an hour before that phone call, I heard two mighty bangs from the study. The cat was outside so there was no natural explanation. I asked about this and was told that it can sound like that when energies come through the realms. I had noticed that before, but then it sounded more like snapping in the room. Now I understood.

Then all the children and grandchildren came. It was very precious and good. We were all at the Memorial Park and we met up close to home. Everyone had their close relationship to Mikael and he was there among us.

The next close soul-meeting with Mikael was particularly delicate. He came to me as a kind of love-wind and to a particularly special place in my heart...

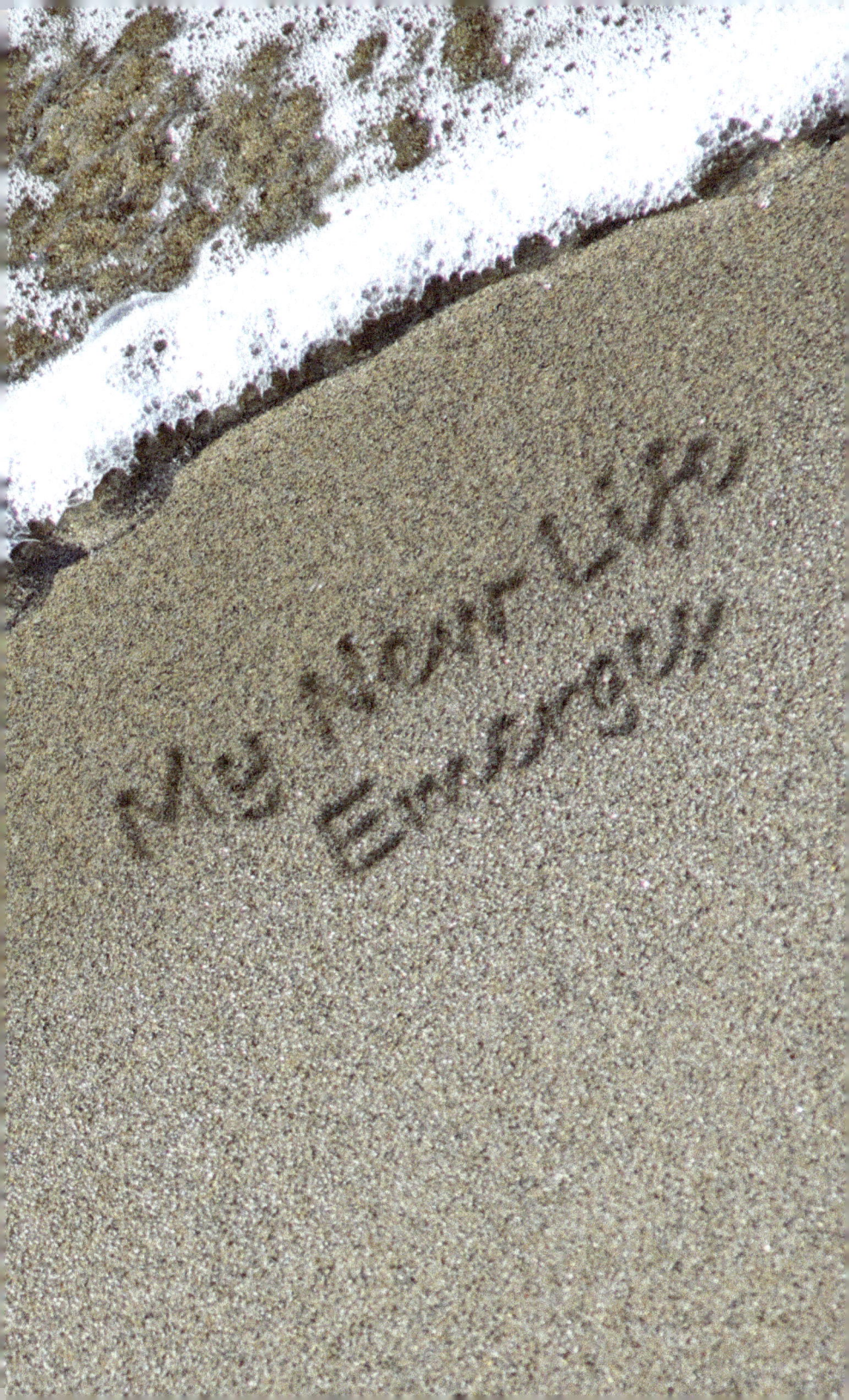

It is now a little more than a year since Mikael left us. Traditionally, but also based on old wisdom, this period is known as the grieving year. Living through an entire year without the one you have lost has a particular meaning. When that first year of grief is concluded, a new life can slowly begin to emerge. To me right now, I feel as if I live my life on parallel tracks. It has been important for me, without Mikael physically by my side, to get through the summer at our beloved summerhouse by the sea, to continue working, to celebrate Christmas and both our birthdays, and above all to go though the anniversary of Mikael's death. At the same time, although being physically apart, we have also developed our marriage in soul during this important year. We have merged our light bodies and hearts. And we now exist in the same field on the energy plane, both here on Earth within me and where Mikael is in the timeless dimensions. In these frequencies there are no distances and only oneness exists.

"One can't live one's life backwards," I happened to say to someone who asked me how my life is now. Afterwards I realised how true that was. Mikael and I have built something together in soul that would not have been possible if he was still here on Earth with me. To me, this has meant breath-taking experiences and glimpses into the mysteries of life, that have both shaken me and filled me with wonder. None of these events would have been possible for me to make up, not even in my wildest imagination. The energies that showed me the way have always turned up when I least expected and turned my usual ways of thinking upside-down. These new learnings, insights and understanding have enriched and changed me and my life incredibly. Still and at the same time, my challenge is to be able to fit this new person that I have become, into a society that often does not acknowledge these kinds of experiences. I still feel I can only confide in very few people.

Throughout my life, I have many times been faced with a crossroad. At these times I have always heard a voice within me asking: *Are you prepared for the next step?* Each time I have answered yes to the question, and done so three times. It has been like an oath to myself above all, but even to those on the Other Side who are there with me. It requires a lot of courage to follow your soul's deepest desire, without any compromises. It is easy to yield towards a path that is more accepted in society. But the soul's deepest desire is our compass. Every soul knows deep inside which direction it should take and will tell you, if you give yourself time and space to listen to this often quiet voice or special inner tone. When I am close or at one with that tone, I feel an extreme joy, lightness and purpose, and when I have failed to follow it, the consequences have been feelings of heaviness and sorrow.

At this time, I feel a need to recharge my batteries. I need to have the energy to express to the outside world, all that I have become in my inner world. To recharge, I normally go on a retreat or in some other way meet people in similar situations, making sure I am surrounded by like-minded people and in a place where we can lift each other. I perceive this as nutrients for body and soul. To me, it is also important that I am there with my entire inner experience without being occupied with what I can reveal or not. To be filled to the brim with unconditional love is a miracle in itself and extra powerful when there is a whole group letting it in. When you have received in this manner it becomes completely natural to allow it to flow forward to others who have not yet received that gift. And in that way, you gain a practical understanding of how everything is connected.

During Easter 2013 I was at a retreat (or the Days of Light). We received what was called "crystal energy", that I think of as Christ energy or unconditional love. It was a continuation of the gift at Christmas with the "crystal egg" which had since developed through soul-meetings between Mikael and me. This crystal egg is now united in all my chakras, which in turn have merged and become one single chakra. During the meditations at the retreat I felt threads of different colours from the crystal egg and I thought of everything that had been created the past months.

Through all this I gained an understanding of how creation and manifestation can come about. Within I could see how my new life was being created around me. I saw my/our new home as a ball of energy in different colours, pulsating with energy. It will be my new spiritual home and it will exist as an extension of the crystal energy that is within me. I/we have been given this opportunity, since we have taken on a mission to contribute to the world by sending out this form of crystal energy.

I spent Easter Monday at home. I needed the whole day to bring down and calibrate everything that had happened during the retreat into my physical body. It turned into a beautiful ceremony where I surrendered myself even more deeply, fully aware that this relates to the man-woman connection in ever higher dimensions.

During the period after Easter 2013 and until the summer, the run-up to my new life intensified on all fronts. The energies increased from the inside and at critical moments I needed to make decisions. It was not just about making a new life. I realised: "I neither can, want to, or am able to live in my old ways." Mikael was very active within me during the process of shaping my, and our, new life. I felt his strong love through my entire being. To me this was such a lovely support and I constantly thanked him.

— You are being made over, being made completely new. You have to let all the old stuff go.

These words came to me in the car one morning, when I was on my way to work and happened after I had taken some important decisions about how my new life should be shaped. The first step was to ask for help with all the practical details of selling the house. Through old habits, I had made myself far too alone with this. A lot needed to be cleaned out before the viewings, which had felt tough on many levels. Help came along, of course, when I communicated clearly about what I needed.

The other thing was my role in the consulting firm. It was time to tell my colleagues about my fragility and how I had changed during the year. I was quite nervous about the meeting, but it turned into a wonderful conversation which allowed me to release my old pattern of being "the last person standing" when it came to holding the company together. The meeting also led to a good decision on my part, as I decided to leave the post as managing director after the summer and only remain as partner.

What ease and joy after this decision! Now I could let go of the responsibility of managing a team in a market that I no longer understood and more importantly, since I had changed so much myself, I no longer wanted to. I felt a great joy that new forces would take over...

In the middle of all the cleaning out and other challenges I had the good fortune to meet a friend for a couple of days, who could understand the great things happening within me. It was obvious that we were important to each other in the forming of our new lives. We shared many happy and releasing bouts of laughter where we easily moved between different dimensions. Soon after these days together I sat by myself in the sofa, no candles lit that time. Instead I saw a special light shining on my left, a new phenomenon for me. It felt like Mikael had plugged into our happy laughter and to the joyful construction of a new life built on spiritual ground in and for a new era.

It was truly time for renewal in all areas, not only in body and soul. Three of four kitchen appliances broke down just before selling, so I had to buy new ones. Even my old car broke down and there was no point trying to get it repaired. I ordered a new car and also got help fixing a new bridge for my teeth, everything was being renewed. My ankle and foot that I had had problems with a few years ago and which still made the rest of my body stiff, also needed attending. I understood that I was being prepared in all areas before 2016 when the new life would be in place.

Mikael was there with me the whole time. As soon as I allowed myself a moment of quiet, he was there tangibly in his energy within my body or dialoguing through the flame of my candle. One afternoon I was sitting and enjoying the sun. I had parked my critical "must-dos" and sat there with the sea in front of me and with the mild spring breeze caressing my cheeks. Then I allowed myself to let go and flew for a while with Mikael. With the help of the birds and nature, as Master Kuthumi had once taught me, it worked like a dream. When I am in that state, Mikael and I come together when I place my focus on my forehead. I met Mikael like that this afternoon and I wanted to know how it was where he was. I asked him and he replied:

– *Like now when you are flying – consciousness without a body (physical).*

There was an ease, joy and such pleasure from flying together. I noticed that I opened up spiritually even more.

146

There were only a couple of months until summer and the renewal of my life had intensified even more. It was very noticeable how active Mikael was in this transformation. We met in different ways day and night. Our inner meetings helped me immensely in all areas, especially when it came to handle all outer things, even if it also meant that I wasn't sleeping very much...

At this time, the renewal of my/our life was beginning to manifest itself, also physically.

At the consulting firm, we had a meeting where everything was up in the air. The pressure created by the lack of activity in our area had caused some anxiety and several of my colleagues were questioning how "professional" we were. How much should we adjust to an old way of thinking and how much of our extreme process-orientated way of working could the market tolerate? The polarisation of the business world had become even clearer to me. Between those who stick to the old ways of business organisation on the one side and those who want to work in a new way on the other. This forced us to take a look at how we marketed ourselves.

My decision to leave as managing director was very well grounded within me. The others understood me and I understood those who are in their mid-life years too. During my entire career, I have been able to be myself and have not needed to fit into any mould that didn't suit me. Maybe that is a luxury in today's society? In the end it boils down to my inner changes, I simply can't force myself to fit into a mould that isn't truly who I am. I felt that my usual enthusiasm and drive was not there anymore. It was as I no longer could understand how the business world functioned. I wanted another type of life – in stillness.

The night after the meeting was very intense. I slept well at first, but high energies woke me up after a few hours and they were flowing into my body through my crown.

My head was very heavy from these energies. My "light hands" were holding on to my tense thigh muscles. The muscles in my thighs had been tense for several weeks, probably due to the conflict between my inner and outer life, which both were so intensive at this time. Moment by moment I kept my focus on the empty space within, as I had been taught. Then the high energies could affect the tense muscles and my light hands steered them in the right direction by touching the muscles. Stepwise the tensions were released and the energies continued to flow undisrupted, the blockages were dissolved.

In the morning, and through the candle flame which was flickering wildly, I had a close soul-meeting with Mikael. While he was still here in the physical world, we often had conversations about how we wanted to live our lives. Now, we continued the discussion in the same uncomplicated fashion. I was strengthened by the realisation that I neither could, nor wanted to live as I did in my old life. My focus was even different when it comes to working. I longed to get time to write Mikael's and my book. Its title came to me: *Love beyond Death.*

The following day we held a seminar at the office. Our consultant group had invited a speaker to moderate the seminar. It was an important day, a new kind of collaboration, and we had external clients that came to participate too. I was there in the morning to help arrange all practical things and then made myself ready to listen. Rather incautiously I had taken a seat in the middle of the room instead of at the back. The energies from above took over without me realising and it looked like I was asleep. It felt impolite and rather embarrassing. A colleague kindly tapped me on the shoulder and I left the room as discretely as I could. I understood that I needed to be alone, when in this state. I sat in a separate room, out of the way of the rest of the group, and received an intense download of high energies that went on for a couple of hours.

To me this all felt as if I had carefully been removed from the seminar and I realised this was another step in the change that was going on. I should no longer be in the middle. I needed to take new steps and take on a completely different role. Towards the end of these intense two hours I heard three knocks at the door. I stood up and opened the door since I thought somebody needed to get hold of me. But nobody was there, so I sat down again. I understood then that the knocking sound had been inside of me and that the knocks represented a question: *Are you prepared for the next stage?* Just like at several earlier occasions when faced with this question I, without a doubt and with great joy, replied "yes" three times. It felt like this represented the official beginning of my new life.

A short while later I could for the first time see the whole room clearly. It had been milky from the high energies, and more so than I had ever experienced. My way of coming back was to go out into the kitchen and take care of the dishes. When the guests had left the building, I was able to speak with my colleagues, apologise and tell them what had happened. Our good sense of companionship meant that everyone understood that this was a transformation that was good for all of us and that it was a part of our new platform.

The morning after I was awakened early, before the alarm went off, by a loud sound in the room. I felt Mikael's presence and knew we had been close together all night. The bang came when I needed to come back to the three-dimensional world. It was analogous to the knocking sounds at the office. A strong, loud sound that was apparently there somewhere in my perception. Marina has told me that different types of sound can occur in the meeting point between the dimensions. I have often heard clicking in the room, and a few times also loud or knocking sounds.

A few days later, a Saturday, I had an experience that was completely earth-shattering and which forever will stay with me. The day before, was the one-year anniversary of Mikael's funeral and of the memorial which we had held in his honour. This fact was important to me. After this first year the new life would be made apparent. When reflecting upon this later, I still have the same feeling.

I had cleaned out the bathroom, put together the medicines that were left and had handed them over to the chemist's. There was so much unnecessary stuff that needed to be cleared, to make the bathroom uncluttered and nice. Getting rid of the medicines was one important step to make sure that Mikael's illness was cleared away from our home. When cleaning out our bathroom I found some bottles of Mikael's aftershave and thought that maybe one of our sons may want them. I went to the chest of drawers in Mikael's room to put them there. When opening the small drawer, I was surprised to find Mikael's wallet there, in some way it must had been moved there from the cupboard. I was a little surprised but left it there. Behind it, in the same drawer, were a few small jewellery cases. I recognised the boxes which used to belong to my mother-in-law. In the two smaller ones were jewellery that Mikael had given to me after my mother-in-law died. In a similar old jewellery case, there was a seemingly completely new bracelet that I had never seen before. Despite the fact we had been going through the chest of drawers and those jewellery cases several times since Mikael's death.

This was such a shock to me. How did that bracelet get there? My mind was in turmoil when I tried to understand with my intellect. Of course, I could not. At first, I ran from the room and hid, shaking all over. Then I calmed down and sat in the armchair beside the chest of drawers and just accepted the gift without having to understand how it had got there. Mikael was there within, and I thanked him.

It was an extremely powerful soul-meeting. Mikael confirmed that the gift was for me, a symbol of our new life together. He reminded me that the funeral was a year ago yesterday. He thanked me for this year, when we had deepened our love even further and he also told me that he had understood how much I loved him, but also how much he loved me. My whole body shook. Could this be possible? I chose just to accept. Then he came to me and filled me completely with energies from my forehead to the base of my spine. With my left hand he caressed my cheeks, tears of happiness and intimacy welled up. *You are my rose...* Yes, so it is. Through the aeons. I sat there a long while and just enjoyed the intimacy.

The bracelet carries a special symbolic value that is connected to the gold heart and also the ring I once bought at the Taj Mahal in India. All these pieces of jewellery have a ruby set in them. Ruby has a particular significance for me spiritually and it has to do with the Christ energy. That is why I bought the ring and why I had the gold heart made with a ruby set into it. The bracelet is in fixed gold, beautifully crafted with a large ruby in the centre surrounded by small diamonds. It looks rather like a large ring. The symbolism reinforces my sense of wonder for what is happening.

In the same box where the bracelet and Mikael's wallet lay, I found our marriage certificate and the christening certificate of our son. There were also pieces of a porcelain figure that was broken. I remember that Mikael was sad about that. It is a figure of a beautiful woman kneeling and looking in a mirror. The day I found the bracelet I tried to repair the porcelain figure and almost succeeded. Two pieces were missing that I found the next day and glued back on. It felt important. Now she is whole and closely connected with Mikael. I am her, and she represents our love and my reply to Mikael.

Two days after I found the bracelet, Mikael came to me with a clear message. I was awakened by my arms tingling with energy. At the same time, I was receiving high energies through my crown and forehead. Mikael was intensely present. Then his voice and words came within:

– *Your arms shall become wings. Everything is possible!!! It is the logic thoughts that limit you. The bracelet is yours. It was placed there and not by physical hands. I can't tell you more now. The bracelet has many meanings, you will understand more as time passes. My love for you is manifest in it. It also acts as a reminder and a protection for you, and a sign that your right-hand side is now totally directed towards the divine plane and our work. You should not be burdened by earthly duties. Then you cannot fly. And you have released a lot now. You are on your way to releasing everything.*

The bracelet symbolises what you embody here on Earth from your spiritual tradition. Now your life will be dedicated to living this here on Earth with me and with our love inside you. It is now time to deliver the message completely, and with the feminine aspect. You are not only motherly but also a genuine woman. Therefore, you should write about our love and of love beyond death. Just as you understood the composition of the ruby stones, you will be able to convey the message.

The imbalance in your body is something you struggle with. On your right-hand side you have in a previous lifetime been stabbed by a bayonet. You were a man and fought with someone, defending a good cause. Get help and you will get to know more.

My left hand placed itself over my right hand on the rib. A deep sense of calm and warmth spread through my body. *We are healing this now...* I heard, and felt that it was so. Images swept past...

Sometime later that day I discovered that time had stopped while Mikael's words had been channelled. In my bedroom, the clock showed 11.25 am while the other clocks in the house were showing 2 pm. The clock in the bedroom was still working. The difference in time was exactly the amount of time it took for me to receive Mikael's message in the bedroom. I have experienced this before, what I call "a gap in time", but never for such a long period.

That night Mikael came to me again and continued to heal me from the injury in my rib. The heat spread through my body. Something ancient was released. My light hands placed themselves over my womb. The heat spread deeply and I received an intimate understanding and love for me as a woman. Mikael's voice said:

– *Your lives as a man has left a fear in you. As a woman in this life you have carried this and have needed to be strong. That has created an imbalance that is now being released.*

I was shivering all day, due to this experience. I felt that Mikael was so close in everything that was happening in this special time. My entire body was being refurbished and I was releasing my old habit of taking on too much responsibility and control. My bracelet helped me even during long work days. I felt the power in it and how much it helped me keep my balance. It was almost like a sort of GPS. This whole thing was so amazing that I was stunned. And it also gave me peace, closeness and joy...

The word "manifesting" has taken on a new meaning for me after I got to experience it for real during the few months of the spring of 2013. Earlier I believed that it was something only spiritual people with great experience and maturity could achieve. On the other hand, I believe that we all manifest each day with our thoughts. We wish for something and visualise it before us. Before we produce anything in writing, drawing or music, there is an inspiration within us that we then express in the particular form of expression that is just right for each individual.

As an experienced Gestalt Therapist, I am very familiar with what we term "the creative space". That means that I consciously need to remain in that space, for something new to be formed. We humans often have difficulty being in uncertainty or an empty space and quickly try filling with thoughts and feelings. These thoughts and feelings are like old garbage which prevent the creative forces from working. The new is in the now moment.

Inspiration means "in spirit", which can be interpreted as; In order for innovation to happen we need insights beyond our day-to-day thoughts. Fear-based feelings inhibit innovation the most. We need to be free so that spiritual insights can come through. So far, I had felt at home with a long career behind me with very much innovation and creativity. However, what I experienced when my new home (or rather our new home, as I perceive it) was being manifested, really shook me and my life was never the same. I found myself in a completely new life.

All these changes took place initially from the inside, then moved outwards and every step was very tangible. My role in this process was a total surrender to Mikael on the Other Side and the higher energies. For his part, it meant that he was with me the whole time in soul, as he had chosen to do. A long time afterwards I understood that after his death, Mikael went up into the light, and chose to wait for me there. All along he has been there for me. Things like this go in stages and it takes longer when we are on Earth compared to when being on the Other Side. I also understood that what we are going through since Mikael's passing, i.e. with me here on Earth and with him on the Other Side, is part of a very old agreement between the two of us.

Along our soul path we, in most cases, only receive glimpses of wisdom and can only see pieces of the whole picture. It can be frustrating, but is necessary for our souls to learn and mature. When I was in the midst of the intensive period when my/our new home was being manifested, I was living in a strong energy field between the physical world's norms and my inner world. This gave me jolts of joy as well as experiences that challenged my ordinary way of viewing the world. There was no mistake that it was for real. My entire body vibrated with energies and I heard words and statements from Mikael on the Other Side that later turned out to be exactly correct predictions regarding how things would progress. Manifestation happens far beyond the intellect.

The bracelet, which came to me in a completely unexpected manner, taught me that there is so much between Heaven and Earth that cannot be explained intellectually. I simply chose not to find any logical explanation and accepted this enormous love-gift from the bottom of my heart. Through the bracelet I was helped to stay focused on my inner world and thereby remain balanced when I moved about in the physical world.

In my inner life with Mikael, our soul-meetings were continuing in ever higher energies, day and night. My light hands lived their own life and moved around, light as feathers, soothing my tense muscles. My physical body became relaxed during our soul-meetings and energy transferred. However, these energies needed to cut through old blockages. The realms can easily clash with each other. During one of these soul-meetings I heard Mikael say:

— *The trick is to keep your balance. You need to be out there. At the same time not drown out there. You are an instrument. What is being healed inside you is being healed for the whole, for humanity. That's why our soul-meetings are so crucial. Your bracelet is the symbol.*

I feel embraced and carried in the midst of my day-to-day duties. The uncertainty of selling our house and getting a new place for me/us was still overwhelming. I viewed some possible places but realised that I first must sell our house. Before that, there was no point looking at any apartments.

My requirements for our new home were roughly like this: "The apartment doesn't need to be big, but light and airy. I want something beautiful to look at, preferably the sea. And I want to live in the same area where I've lived for more than 30 years, which is near the sea." What I didn't know was that my wishes would be more than fulfilled.

During all this I visited my clairvoyant friend Doris. As usual I didn't give her any information about what was going on inside me, but she saw Mikael close to me straight away. She saw him place his hands on my shoulders and say that he was proud of me. He described this to Doris and she saw that we were closer than ever. That agreed with my experience. It's like we were let free to love and be loved when our earthly constraints were released.

Doris continued:

— He is wearing a working shirt today with the sleeves rolled up. He is showing that he is actually with you, completely present with everything that is going on right now. Both your move and your work at the consulting firm. When the peonies bloom you will have a buyer.

If what Doris said was true, then I would have a buyer at the end of June and be able to move in August. Could that be possible? In the garden, there is a scented pink peony that blooms in the beginning of the summer. However, there is also another dark pink peony that flowers later at the end of June, which also was the peony that became "my flower" when I met Justo for an individual session in 2008. The summer after that session I went through what is termed "the inner marriage" on the energy plane, that is to say a union of my male and female aspect at the energy level. Very powerful and wonderful! And a prerequisite for what I am experiencing now with Mikael.

The next day my soul-meeting with Mikael was even more powerful. The "crystal egg" was vibrating and Mikael approached from my crown and the base of my spine. Everything was united in energy in a sort of conception. The experience was connected to the two embryos that I felt were created in the energy in connection with the journey to Titicaca. These embryos were united with the crystal egg and now it was fertilised both from above and below, at that the same time. To me it felt like the creation of a love child in soul energy. Then it calmed down and I was carefully embraced. It took a long while to return to our normal third dimension. It was getting light outside and I lay there for ages, my body warm and soft, full of wonder and gratitude. Just like with the bracelet, I allowed these experiences to be a gift, knowing that it was beyond the intellect.

During this time, I started to get a hint of what it means to manifest. That, which is to be created physically on Earth is first created on the energy plane just like when we create something with the power of thought. The key is, as in everything, love, gratefulness and release. The power of love is the same as the creative force. That is why it is love that holds the universe together. We create our universe through our desire and love, and thereby become the instrument and intermediary for that which is later manifested on Earth on the physical plane. You could say that we are creators and receivers in the same being and this is particularly powerful in the cooperation between dimensions. That is, when we on Earth are given access to higher energies.

During the creative process, Doris explained, lines or links can be created. From my experiences during this intensive spring, I can see that a timeline is at work. At the end of March, it was Mikael's birthday and two days after this the anniversary of his death. I chose to go to Sturebadet, a spa in central Stockholm, for some leisure time and to remember Mikael and his family. I felt an extra closeness by being there. One month later, on the 27th of April, the day after the anniversary of Mikael's funeral, I received the bracelet. His words to me then, and how he emphasised that one year had passed and that during that year since his death he had truly understood how much I love him, and how much he loves me, were all very clear and close to me.

At the end of May the energy was built up again. In one of our many inner soul-meetings Mikael placed words on my tongue. He does so when it is extra important.

— The meetings in our light bodies are our way of creating and manifesting. Our intertwined light bodies need to be connected to your physical body so that manifestation can take place on Earth. Never forget who you are in your soul!!! It is not boasting – it is your responsibility and a prerequisite for what we are going to create.

A couple of hours later I woke up with big muscle-aches. I sought temporary help from painkillers and went back to sleep. When I woke up in the early morning a new intimate soul-meeting took place. This time I was shown my throat chakra very vividly, and how it was interconnected to all the other chakras. Once again Mikael put his words on my tongue:

— We manifest now our move (three times), we manifest now that our house is sold (three times) we manifest now our new house (three times). All of this is for finding our platform in the new life. The platform, for that which shall be created and manifested.

Two days later, I was once again on my way to Sturebadet. On my way in the train, Mikael came to me again. I had been rather hesitant about wearing the bracelet but I heard a clear voice from Mikael: - I will be with you! And he was with me. My left hand (Mikael) held the bracelet protectively the whole journey. Once again I heard Mikael's voice:

— Now you are the person the bracelet symbolises. See the world from there. Not with your old eyes. I am with you.

It was not entirely pleasant to see the world in this way. I felt a great deal of affection for other people but things that happened seemed foreign to me. I didn't want to find myself there. During the past few weeks I had observed elderly couples and the thought had crossed my mind that it could have been Mikael and me. That had passed by and I no longer wanted that. I did not wish to lose the loving company that had developed between us the last year.

I had my hours of pleasure at the Sturebaded Spa. It felt somewhat like a cleansing before entering my new life. My bracelet was very safely hidden away in my favourite cardigan. On the train on my way home, Mikael came back to me:

– *You are undergoing such a great transformation that you feel lost regarding who you are. It's a new identity for you. You can easily confuse your feeling of being lost identity-wise, with feelings of grief for me. Mostly it is rather that you step by step are leaving your, and my, old life on all fronts. You will be able to start living as you have thought, but in a few years, you will not be living in Sweden. By then you will have found a group of people with whom you want to live and where my presence is natural.*

This is a whole new identity but it is emerging gradually. You will end up leaving everything in your current life as well as your current lifestyle. It will more be more like living in a convent, but not really that either.

You and I are shaping a completely new life. The bracelet is the symbol of that, of who you are in that new life. We take with us the love we have fostered in our physical life together, but also what we have learnt. However, this new life is connected to other previous lives we have had of a higher, more spiritual nature. You are doing something very special by staying behind on Earth, at the same time as you on a soul level are merging with me on the Other Side. Our shared plan. You are now in the midst of your transformation and the new life is starting to take over clearly. Nurture and go into your new identity. We will meet there and build. In a month, everything will be sorted out with the house and you can calmly go to our summer house and enjoy life. You can see the timeline yourself for your visits to Sturebadet and that has been very meaningful. See the symbolism of that and enjoy!

Thank you, my darling Mikael! You knew that I needed your help and your strength now. I will relax in the sun chair and remain in the flow. I understand more when you show that the new is connected with the previous lives we have shared. I also remember when you said on our way into town: *Your love is the base for everything. You penetrated the shell I had around me.* I replied inside myself that I also bore a shell back then. True, you said, but it is still your love that has opened me up.

I have always loved Mikael since we first met. I was grateful for that love every day and all those years. I felt his love so strongly even when the fear was present as well. Those last years when Mikael was with us here on Earth, I felt an abundance within, from all the unconditional love I had received during my inner journey with Master Kuthumi. In turn, I was led there by my soul brother L. The collaboration between the three of us is very special. I can see that there is much more to it than the mere glimpses I have seen this far.

The following day I was contacted again, this time when on the underground. I felt it was as if my bracelet was a sort of satellite navigation. I heard these words from Mikael:

– *You are right in the midst of your preparations for your new identity. Today you have crossed the threshold. Your new identity has grown and moved in, and will take over all the more. A completely new life.*

The day after those two overwhelming days, I found myself in a kind of vacuum and as usual I needed to deal with blockages in my physical body as well as one or two practical matters.

I went for a long walk and was helped by Mother Nature to release old issues that were in my way. Late that evening Mikael and I met through a wildly flickering candle flame and an intense high energy entered me through the crown and into my whole body. It moved with life and strength and brushed aside the feelings of heaviness. My left hand (Mikael) was placed over my wrist where the bracelet usually was placed, on my right arm. I understood that it was Mikael helping me through this strange day. Then these words came:

– *You need this empty space so that the transformation can take place in a good way.*

Of course, I can see that now. The creative vacuum is necessary. And I should not fill it with worry or meaningless things. I need to have courage to be there consciously. Thank you, Mikael, my love! Time to sleep now.

After this the week was denoted by uncertainty about utter things, as the sale of the house and my upcoming move. For this whole period, I was aided from within, not to be carried away by worry or to get stuck in situations that lead nowhere. It was obvious that I should be in this empty space and be very aware that I was there. Mikael and I met day and night in our light bodies. In that way, I was helped to maintain my peace through accepting what it all was about:

– *You are not primarily selling a house – you are building a whole new life.*

164

These words from Mikael helped me to avoid getting stuck in details, but rather ensure that I kept myself in high energies, free from worry. I prayed to the highest within me to show me the way. And once again I confirmed my readiness to go into my new identity that already had begun to move into my physical body.

Towards the end of the vacuum-week, during which I was tested and understood that I needed to pronounce my readiness and my commitment to the new life that was coming, I felt a release. Once again, I was filled with those high energies, which lasted for many hours. These words from Mikael came to me:

— *Now we are manifesting the new life, the platform we need to live it.*

I had now learnt and I understood with all my soul and physical body how things happened in our soul-meetings. Mikael also showed his presence by moving the porcelain figure that I had pieced back together when I had found the bracelet. To me it was like a greeting from him.

Then the day came when we had a buyer for the house, and the same day I went to see the apartment that I really wanted to buy. In some way, both had conspired to happen on the same Sunday! When I walked up the hill to my new apartment, tears came before I even saw it. The same thing happened when I stepped in. There it was, not so big, surrounded by nature and with a wonderful view over the sea, just as I had dreamt it should be. It is one of five apartments in a house from the turn of the previous century, light and with high ceilings.

The following days were strange. Everything seemed to fall into place. The buyers of the house were happy, I was content with my new apartment. Nonetheless there was a lot that needed to be done for everything to be finalised. I needed to be assured that I wouldn't get stuck in worry or fixed ideas about the future. I needed to be satisfied but not get stuck in the dream either. Once again help came from within, powerfully and lifted me over the actual transactions.

I came to think of what Mikael had said at the end of May:

— *Everything will be ready by the end of June. You can then go to the summer house and relax.*

Also, Doris had said to me in May when I was visiting: *You will have a buyer when your peonies are in bloom.*

Now in the middle of June the peonies are in bud and just waiting to blossom. The contracts are signed both for our house sale and for buying the new apartment. Of course, the one depends upon the other. It remains before everything is finalised to organise the actual date for paying the deposit and surveys and so on.

I get to experience a special Midsummer celebration. I am learning to be without needs, still being true to my dreams. Among other things this concerned being firm on the price I set on the house. Take it or leave it! I thank my spirit guides and especially Mikael who taught me how to prepare for the worst and at the same time believe in the best of outcomes. I also learned to ask for help from my physical family and to remember that the focus is on building a completely new life, not primarily about selling a house.

Our soul-meetings during the Midsummer weekend meant that we were manifesting this last piece of creating a platform for our new life. The feeling was so clear and it gave me strength. Once again I was reminded of the words I had heard:

— Focus upon our inner union – not outside events. They are a consequence of our union.

The day after Midsummer the deal was sealed and finally the remaining butterflies could leave my stomach. Two days later the deposit was in place in my bank account and I could pay the deposit for the new apartment. The same afternoon as the deposit was in my account, the peony in my garden flowered. A couple of days later I was at our summer cottage by the sea and I could relax for several weeks and build up strength for the actual move.

Our new home is to be the base for our completely new life, where we will continue to cooperate between the worlds. I have no idea how this is going to look. My mission here on Earth is to keep myself open and free and thus to allow higher powers the space to act within me. Spiritual energies lift us to great heights when we allow ourselves to receive them. At the same time, the spirit world needs our hands and feet. It is all about the actual collaboration.

Thank you, Mikael, and my other guides on the Other Side! What an amazing lesson I had in the art of manifesting. And so much love along the way...

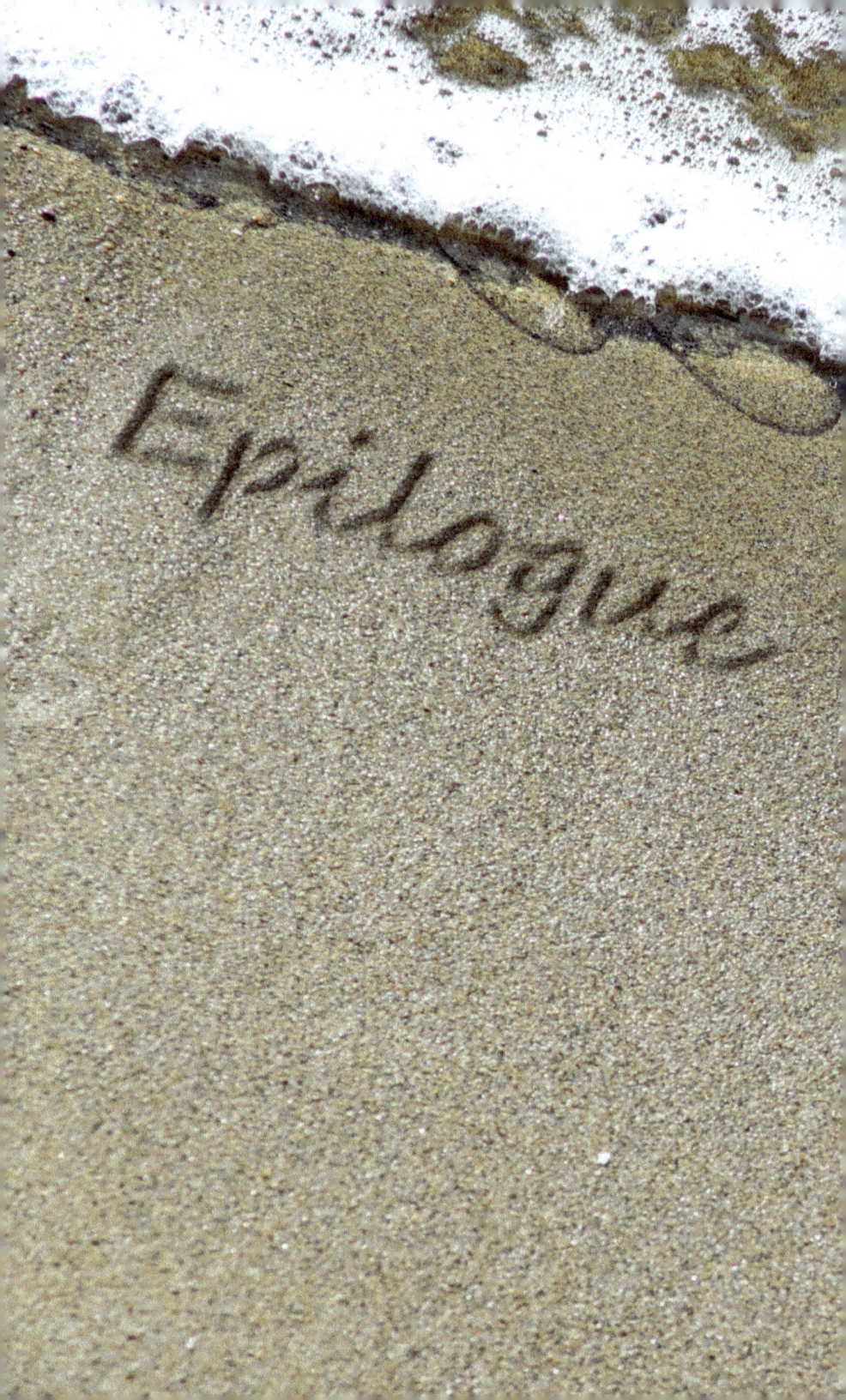

Epilogue

My story spans approximately one and a half years and describes my experiences both without and within since Mikael's death. It is about my grief for the man of my life, but above all about how love overpowers death.

Love Beyond Death was first published in Swedish in 2016. That is no coincidence. I had for a long time been told from within that our new life together would come to fruition in this year. The years leading up to 2016 have been preparations. Those years have been full of inner loving soul-meetings between us, which brought us ever closer together. Simultaneously I, as the one who is still on Earth, have been supported in leaving all that weighs me down in the outside world. You need to be light in order to fly.

The path I have chosen is filled with love and I am deeply grateful for having been led into it in several steps, as I described at the beginning of the book. This unconditional love is there for us all and just waiting for us to let it in. It sounds so simple, receiving love, but at the same time it awakens everything that we have not received earlier in life. And we may have a hard time accepting that we are loved by the creative force which one time created us.

My conviction is that there is a divine spark in every human being. That seed has been nourished through many different lives to mature. I think of this part of us as a tone or an essence that is unique to each and every one. When we remember and come close to this tone we experience a lightness of being and often a desire to explore more of it. It is up to us to choose if we want to feed our divine spark more in this life or not. Nobody is chosen. We ourselves choose our path. Help comes when we have made our choices.

My wish is that you, the reader, look upon my/our story as an example of what can happen when the soul gets to fly more freely. You have followed me in the reasoning that this is not to be taken for granted, rather freedom comes in stages. Longing for this freedom is the force that leads to the soul coming to bloom here on Earth. Everyone has their path. The flourishing and the ways of flourishing are different. We each have our unique mission, as I see it.

Why am I here? Where do I come from? Where am I headed? These three questions have their place in most philosophies and religions. They are existential and are present in our lives, especially during tough times. In our day-to-day existence, the noise often tends to take over. But when we lose a loved one through death or separation, when we deal with our illness or near death, or when we for some reason do not get to live the life we dreamt of, it is then these questions come to us. And we search for answers...

Eben Alexander, a neurosurgeon, who himself was close to dying, wrote about this. He writes that traditional science cannot answer these questions. Science gives us a lot, but not the answers to life's most central questions. He expresses through his book the soul's perspective for exploring these questions.

The concept "the dark night of the soul" concerns when we stand there and still have not dared to believe that we each carry a spark of the divine within us, a spark that wishes to blossom. My experience is that we need to express our desire and wish to be close to our soul and the divine spark. Then and only then we receive help. Just as it is for us on Earth, the divine world cannot just walk in without us wishing it. How can they know if we don't ask for help?

We can all start by expressing our desire and our need to the highest within us. What we call this highest aspect is not relevant as I see it. If the term God is muddied by different peoples' interpretations, we can pray to the Creative force, or to Universal love. We are anyhow linked with the energy that we pray to. Everything is part of the whole.

"Spiritual seeker" has become a concept. I was myself one for most of my life. That changed when I at long last realised that the key is to come to a standstill and instead become an increasingly more sensitive *receiver* for that unconditional love, which is there all the time for everybody, and allow it into every cell.

We can begin by bathing in the rays of the sun. The sun spreads light on us all and doesn't judge. We can choose to allow the sun in or not. We can take in all of nature in the same manner, or not. It is there for us all. We can allow in the life we have been given and the miracle of it. Even during hard times, we have in fact been given a life to live and nurture. When we receive and take in, we are filled with gratitude even for apparently tiny things. Gratitude makes us free...

Above nature itself, I and many others have found that there are people who have gone before us and opened the way. Both here on Earth and beyond we have the possibility to receive love and guidance in this way. It occurs through resonance, we receive and exchange on a wavelength where it is possible to meet.

I hope that Mikael's and my book will inspire others to discover and experience that there is love for all of us and that love survives death. It is ultimately that which

172

pushes me to write. If you have had the grace of receiving the love that is meant for all of us, you will be filled with gratitude. The only thing that love requires is just that, to teach that it is there for each and every one of us.

Literature that has inspired

Alexander, E. (2012). *Proof of Heaven – A Neurosurgeon´s Journey into the Afterlife.* London, UK: Piatkus

Alexander, E. (2014). *The Map of Heaven: How Science, Religion, and Ordinary People Are Proving the Afterlife.* London, UK: Piatkus

Botkin, A. L. (2005). *Induced After Death Communication.* Charlottesville, VA, USA: Hampton Roads Publishing

Braden, G. (2008). *The Divine Matrix: Bridging Time, Space, Miracles, and Believes.* Carlsbad, CA, USA: Hay House Inc.

Chopra, D. (2006). *Life After Death: The Burden of Proof.* London, UK: Harmony/Penguin-Random House

Crowley, J. (2012). *Soul Body Fusion: The Missing Piece for Healing and Beyond.* Greenwood Village, CO, USA: Stone Tree Publishing

Eadie, B. J. (1992). *Embraced by the Light.* Placerville, CA, USA: Gold Leaf Press

Heartsong, C. (2002). *Anna Grandmother of Jesus: A Message of Wisdom and Love.* London, UK: Hay House London Ltd

Kenyon, T. & Sion, J. (2002). *The Magdalen Manuscript: The Alchemies of Horus & the Sex Magic of Isis.* Orcas, WA, USA: ORB Communications

Melchizedek, D. (1999). *The Ancient Secret of The Flower of Life (Vol. 1&2).* Flagstaff, AZ, USA: Light Technology Publishing

Melchizedek, D. (2003). *Living in the Heart.* Flagstaff, AZ, USA: Light Technology Publishing

Melchizedek, D. (2007). *Serpent of Light: Beyond 2012 – The movement of Earth's Kundalini and the Rise of the Female Light, 1949 – 2013.* San Francisco, CA, USA: Red Wheel/Wieser

Moody, A., R. (2001). *Life after Life.* New York City, NY, USA: HarperCollins Publisher

Prakasha, P. A. (2009). *The Power of Shakti.* Toronto, Canada: Destiny Books

Prakasha, P. A. (2010). *The Nine Eyes of Light.* Berkley, CA, USA: North Atlantic Books

Prakasha, P. A. & Prakasha, A. A. (2011). *Womb Wisdom.* Toronto, Canada: Destiny Books

Sandker, J-P. (2013). *The art of hearing heartbeats.* New York City, NY, USA: Other Press LLC

Whitworth, E. E. (1980). *Nine Faces of Christ.* Seattle, WA, USA: Wieschmann Publishing

Books published only in Swedish

Hasselqvist-Ax, S. (2014). *Inga fler tårar.* Mörkö, Sweden: LightSpira

Linder, B. (2011). *Jag tog inte mitt liv – jag lämnade bara kroppen.* Västerås, Sweden: Solrosens Förlag

The first version of *Love Beyond Death* was published in Swedish in 2016. The book release that followed, was a party to celebrate my new life and I also wished to thank all who in different ways had been contributing to the birth of the book. Now in 2018 when we publish Love Beyond Death, the production team is slightly different.

When I wish to express my thanks, I see before me my family, many dear friends, my close colleagues and other fellow passengers on my spiritual journey. In the midst of daily life, you helped life to be lighter and easier to live. Thank you for all the support when my life was swaying! In the particular work with producing *Love Beyond Death*, I would especially like to express thanks to a few people.

Doris Ankarberg
Your sharp and clear clairvoyance had been an invaluable help for my previous book *Head in Heaven*. Therefore it was natural for me to turn to you a couple of months after Mikael's death. You were there for me, in understanding the feeling of being like a person cut in a halves after having lost the man of my life. You conveyed Mikael's presence and words just as clearly from the Other Side. It was a relief and it made me trust what I myself was experiencing. Thank you!

Niklas Curman
You have created the pictures in front of each chapter. You have a natural feel for how the pictures will amplify the message of the book. It is a pleasure to be able to work with you in putting the book together as a whole. Besides being family it has been an extra joy working together. Thank you!

Jo Holmberg-Hansson
You are the translator and editor of the English version of *Love Beyond Death*. You are a unique talent in doing this

delicate work and I am forever grateful that you offered me to accomplish this. Your professional background within Psychology is solid and you are well trained within English speaking environments outside Sweden. However, even more valuable concerning this kind of book, is that you also are my close soul friend. Besides translating words and sentences, you have succeeded in bringing the special kind of energy from the Swedish book to English. Thank you!

Ulla Lindgren
You have been part of the team that translated my inner images to the cover of the book. As an artist and soul friend you helped to create a design of the book to make the energy and message visible and expressed to other people. You work with great enthusiasm and joy. Thank you!

Marina Munk
Mikael and I met you in the early 1980's. Then there was a long gap when you were in the Amazon, even if we visited you there for a few weeks in the middle of the 1990's. You returned to Scandinavia and now Sweden in 2009. Soon afterwards we met again during a phase when I was in great need of help and guidance. For many years I have regularly visited you for individual consultations and in different groups. You were also my travel guide for the journeys to Tibet, Peru/Bolivia and Egypt. All of this has been decisive for being able to lift myself to those energies where Mikael and I can meet and develop together. Thank you!

Ivo Mutter
The very day the Swedish book was released was a great day in many ways. I wanted to invite friends that felt natural to be there for Mikael and me in that fragile and great moment. And I wished for you to contribute with

your very special and powerful song and music. In your loving way you held the space. Thank you!

Katarina Persson
We met in the summer of 2015 when I was going through what I called my "trial by fire". It was the start of a journey where Mikael's and my soul relationship was given support that opened us even more to life's mysteries. Your incredible breadth of working so naturally in the universal realm while at the same time keeping both your feet on the ground has allowed me to relax and appreciate the greatness of it all. Thank you!

The Seven Group
You were my close colleagues that followed and supported me in my day-to-day life through Mikael's death, funeral and all that happened since. Few workplaces would have cared for me as you did. I could be myself with you all in the roller-coaster of life. You have been like a warm embrace to me. Thank you!

Justo Viscarra
As a naturalist practitioner from the Aymara tribe, trained in traditional Bolivian medicine, you helped me as early as in 2008 to "find my flower". A lot later on, I understood that it had to do with the "Inner marriage", that is to say to unite the masculine and feminine principles within me. You of all people have the history and power of the Andes within you. You were close to Mikael and me in our inner soul-meetings by The Lake Titicaca. Thank you!

Marie Örnesved
You were my "midwife" when *Head in Heaven* was published. You helped me to even begin thinking of publishing my fragile innermost self through the book. You also helped Mikael to reach out with his message

through his books. How well you know us both. When it was time to publish our joint book it felt natural that you were there with us again. And now publishing *Love Beyond Death* you do the actual hands-on work. In a joyful team-work you find ways to express my message in the design of the book. Thank you!

making **messages** from
loving hearts
available to a **global** audience

cocreators @lightspira.com
www.lightspira.com